G000022626

Dear Dan...
Apologies From an Imperfect World

Dear Dan...
Apologies From an Imperfect World

by Dan Woog

alyson books
los angeles | new york

MANUFACTURED IN THE UNITED STATES OF AMERICA.

THIS TRADE PAPERBACK ORIGINAL IS PUBLISHED BY ALYSON PUBLICATIONS,
P.O. BOX 4371, LOS ANGELES, CALIFORNIA 90078-4371
DISTRIBUTION IN THE UNITED KINGDOM BY TURNAROUND PUBLISHER SERVICES LTD.,
UNIT 3, OLYMPIA TRADING ESTATE, COBURG ROAD, WOOD GREEN,
LONDON N22 6TZ, ENGLAND.

FIRST EDITION: APRIL 2001

00 01 02 03 04 a 10 9 8 7 6 5 4 3 2 1

ISBN 1-55583-553-8

LIBRARY OF CONGRESS CATALOGING-IN-PUBLICATION DATA
WOOG, DAN, 1953–
DEAR DAN... : APOLOGIES FROM AN IMPERFECT WORLD / BY DAN WOOG.—1ST ED.
ISBN 1-55583-553-8
1. HOMOSEXUALITY—HUMOR. 2. GAY WIT AND HUMOR. I. TITLE.
PN6231.H57 W66 2001
816'.6—DC21   00-067538

COVER DESIGN BY PHILIP PIROLO.

Dedication

To everyone—gay or straight—with a sense of humor. To
survive in today's world, you'll need it.

Contents

As an openly gay writer on a variety of gay issues, I get mail. The majority is praise: "Thanks for helping me get the courage to come out" or "I enjoyed your explanation of an issue I never thought about before." That sort of thing. Of course, I receive my share of hate mail too. What is most remarkable is that nearly everyone who objects to something sends me (anonymously, of course) a Xerox copy of my offending piece, filled with arrows, underlines, and exclamation points in red Magic Marker, and either the suggestion that I perform an anatomically impossible yet intriguing-to-contemplate act or the warning that I will burn in hell.

So a couple of years ago I was stunned to receive a letter consisting of only four words:

Dear Dan,
I apologize.

That was it, in its entirety. Two lines. Four words. Seven syllables. Written in blue pen, on lined paper, it was Hemingwayesque in its simplicity, Lincolnian in its eloquence, and Shakespearean in its impact.

Who had written such a note? I had no clue. There was no signature, no return address; even the postmark was smudged.

My mind raced. Could it have been a student who, during one of my frequent talks to high school classes, sat snickering in back, or perhaps said something out of earshot to a friend as they walked out the room? Could it have been a straight person who once made homophobic comments about me, then discovered that a close friend or relative was gay? Could it have been a closeted lesbian who now regrets that in trying to "pass" she made cutting remarks about my writing? Could it have been someone who actually sent me an anonymous letter? Or could it have been a person who had no previous contact with me but singled me out as a representative of the entire gay community?

It could have been any one of those people, or none. It could have been someone I see every day or someone I have never met. It could have been any human being on earth.

The more I thought about that letter, the more I realized: In the course of our lives we all make mistakes. We all say and do stupid things. We all have many reasons to apologize. Some of us actually make those apologies; most of us never quite manage to get around to it.

Certainly, anyone who has ever uttered an antigay comment owes an apology. However, those of us in the gay community have apologies to make too; we hold no monopoly on righteousness. So I decided to write some apologies myself—to and from various groups, inside the gay community and out.

Dear Dan...Apologies From an Imperfect World is, of course, a work of fiction. None of the apologies in this book have been uttered. Yet. Some are funny; some are poignant. All, I hope, are thought provoking.

And wouldn't it be nice if even one of them came true?

Dan Woog
www.danwoog.com
Westport, Conn.
April 2001

Barney Fag
Proceedings on the Floor of the
House of Representatives

Mr. Frank:

I yield to the gentleman from Texas.

Mr. Armey:

I thank the gentleman from Massachusetts.
I rise today to explain my words, which, I regret to say, have been misinterpreted by some.
In slipping my tongue—I mean, in a slip of my tongue—I recently referred to the gentleman from Massachusetts, my distinguished colleague Barney Frank, as "Barney Fag." It has come to my attention that this inadvertent error has been seen by some as malicious, mean-spirited, deliberate, even homophobic. Nothing could be further from the truth. I meant no disrespect to Congressman Faggot—that is to say, Congressman Frank.
Words are funny things. They are made up of vowels and condoms—I mean, consonants—and while they are only symbols, they wield very real power. Words can heal, and words can hurt. We are all aware of the saying, "The penis mightier than the sword"—I mean, "The pen is mightier than my sword"—than "the sword." And consider the child's expression, "Sticks and stones may break my boner, but names can never squirt me." Or something along those lines. I am sure you get my point.
The gentlewoman—rather, the gentleman—from Massachusetts, has a well-respected member on his body—that is to say, is a well-respected member of this body. He has been an effective voice for his potty—his party, I should say—and is highly regarded by the voters of his district, who have stood behind him erection after erection—excuse me, election after election—sending him back to Congress even after such pickadildos—er, peccadilloes—as allowing a male hustler to run a prostitution ring out of his townhouse. That, ladies and genitalmen, is a true testicle—pardon me, testament—to the high esteem in which the voters of the Fey State—that is to say, the Bay State—hold my good friend Bonnie—rather, Barney—Frank.
My dear colleagues, though the distinguished gentleman

from Massachusetts and I might be considered strange bedfellows, we are in truth two birds of a feather who do
indeed flock together. Our home states, though thousands
of miles apart, are in truth quite similar. If I may be
permitted to blow myself—to blow my horn—a bit, the great
state of Texas is known throughout the world as the home
of the Alamo. In 1836 more than 140 men fought valiantly,
shooting until they were spent from exhaustion, in defi-
ance of men who would shove another way of life down their
throats. Over a century and a half later, I know that every
citizen of Massachusetts is justifiably proud of the great
resort town of Provincetown, shining family jewel of Cape
Cod. Every day, I am told, men there exhibit similar kin-
ship and camaraderie, standing shoulder-to-shoulder and
beating off those who would attack their lifestyle.

Like Congressman Femme—Congressman Frank, that is—I
stand firmly in defense of the principles my constituents
hold dear. In Massachusetts they have plunged forward with
programs for young gays and have even pledged taxpayer
dollars to ensure that those perverts—or rather, pupils—
have equal rights to safe schools. When I go down in
Texas—to Texas—I find that we are just as committed to the
concept of equal rights for young hunters. We believe that
every child, whatever his race, religion, ethnic background—hell, even his sexual preference—has the right to
own a gun and kill whatever he wants.

Of course, we disagree on certain issues, as befitting
men who come on—er, come to—different parties. I am, for
example, opposed to abortion. The gentleman from
Massachusetts has said of my side, "Sure, they're pro-
life. They believe life begins at conception and ends at
birth." While I do not believe Congressman Fa—Frank who
has no children, should mock the beliefs of those of us
who do, I respect his and other baby killers' rights to
say what they wish. After all, the First Amendment is one
of the most cherished principles of the Constitution, second only to the Second Amendment, which gives citizens the
right to bear arms. The gentleman from Massachusetts would
like the right to bare everything else too, but that is
not the issue here.

The issues that bind my esteemed colleague and I together are far more important than what pries us apart. We both
shoot from the hip—figuratively speaking, of course. We
are both intensely interested in military affairs, even
though my interest rests in the area of national defense,
while his is in allowing buttfu—I mean, gay servicepeo-
ple—to serve next to normal human beings. And I know that
despite our differences, we both have held each other, and
will continue to hold each other, in the highest regard.

Thank you. I yield back to the gentleman from Massachusetts—and let me get this straight—Barney Frank.

Mr. Frank:

Thank you, Congressman Armey. In the spirit of reconciliation and collegiality, I am prouder than ever to be able to refer to you by the name by which your friends on the Republican side of the aisle know you. It is indeed a pleasure to call you "Dick."

Dear Dale
A Letter From a Mother to Her Daughter

Dear Dale:

Today is the first anniversary of the day you told me you are a lesbian. I've made some stupid mistakes since then, and I hope you'll forgive me. It has not been easy, but I think I'm making progress. Take the first line of this letter, for instance: I wrote "lesbian" without crying. That may not seem like much to you, but to me it's a huge step!

I'm sorry I almost crashed the car when you told me the news. Swerving onto the sidewalk was not the best way to show I still loved you. But I'm sure you realize the news took me by surprise.

I'm sorry the first thing that flashed through my mind was a big softball player with short hair. I should have realized you're not like that: You love your hair long, and you hate softball. We all have our stereotypes, and it was silly of me to think you had suddenly changed and now loved softball.

I'm also sorry that when you brought your girlfriend B. J. home, I started talking about stereotypes and how silly it is to think that lesbians love softball. You probably should have told me she plays first base! I'm glad she took my remark with grace and good humor, even though I felt like a complete idiot.

I'm sorry I sent you to a psychiatrist. I thought you wanted to change, and I was sure she could change you. Now I realize you didn't need to change at all— I needed to. And that she couldn't have changed you even if you'd wanted her to.

I'm sorry I told you how disappointed I was that you'd never give me grandchildren. At the time I had no idea how many lesbians are having children. You corrected me gently, but then I made that remark about "real" grandchildren. That was so thoughtless—especially when you reminded me that your brother and his wife adopted their two.

I'm sorry I told you not to tell your grandmother you are a lesbian because it would kill her. I've been looking in the obituaries for a year now, and I still haven't seen "Esther So-and-So died yesterday at 84. She dropped dead the moment her granddaughter announced she is a lesbian." To be totally honest, I didn't want Nana to know because I thought it would kill me.

I'm sorry that, even though you gave me brochures and phone numbers and information, I did not go to a PFLAG meeting as soon as you came out. I was so scared I would see someone I knew; I never even realized they would be there for the same reason I was! If I had started going to meetings right away, I am sure I would be much further along in my journey today.

Finally, dear, I am most sorry for my first sentence the day you came out. I remember it so clearly: I said, "Why are you doing this to me?" I have since figured out that your lesbianism isn't about me; it's about you. And I have also figured out that it isn't even about being a lesbian at all; it's simply about being the happiest, most fulfilled person you can be.

So happy first anniversary, darling. Thanks for sharing an important part of your life with me. You're my daughter, and I'm proud of you. I know you're proud of yourself too. I hope you'll tell the whole world.

Just don't do it in a moving car.

Love,
Mom

How Dare You Say Our Promotional Materials Are Gay?
Abercrombie & Fitch

To our valued customers:

It has come to our attention that certain recipients of our catalogs—as well as a portion of those who view our advertisements, in-store promotional posters, and even our shopping bags—believe these materials contain homoerotic content.

Nothing could be further from the truth.

Since our founding, it has been our policy to portray Abercrombie & Fitch male models in a variety of settings that all men can relate to. We believe it is perfectly natural for a half dozen buffed, smooth, and very tan young men to cavort in a shower; to grinningly pull down one young man's boxers; to leap joyfully onto one another's shoulders for no apparent reason; to stare longingly at each other while holding a ukelele; to walk, arms around each other's naked torsos, on an otherwise deserted beach. We think it is perfectly normal for two young men with mussed-up hair to be tying their shoes at exactly the same moment.

The fact that so few of our models wear shirts simply reflects our emphasis on sales of other types of apparel, such as boxer shorts and briefs. We should also point out that women appear in some of our catalog photographs and advertisements—although sometimes their heads are not shown, and even when they are, the male-to-female ratio is similar to that found in bars with names like The Ramrod.

Our target audience is *all* male consumers. We believe that all men, straight as well as gay, appreciate the opportunity to pay $12 a year for merchandising materials filled with enticing Bruce Weber photographs of chiseled male bodies, not always even wearing the clothes we purport to sell.

Finally, concerning the T-shirt in our fall catalog that displayed the name of a fictional college athletic team, "the Roosters," along with the slogan "Loud and Proud": Any connection with the term "gay pride," and any association of roosters with any other name for that animal, is purely coincidental.

Once again, we reiterate that our promotional materials are not homoerotic. We are committed to providing high-quality eye candy to men of *all* sexual orientations. Thank you for shopping Abercrombie & Fitch.

The Doctor's Misdiagnosis

CALLER: Hi, Dr. Laura, I've listened to you a long time. I never thought I'd be calling.

DR. LAURA: No one ever does.

CALLER: I'd like some advice.

DR. LAURA: That's what I'm here for! I'm happy to help. Shoot!

CALLER: OK. We've been together for seven years now. We're as in love as we were the day we met. We complement each other perfectly—intellectually, emotionally, and spiritually. And, of course, we're very compatible sexually.

DR. LAURA: Doesn't sound like a problem to me! Seems to me you're a lucky man!

CALLER: No, no, I know, that's not the problem. I'm getting to that.

DR. LAURA: You don't know how many people would love a marriage like yours.

CALLER: Yeah, well, it's not a marriage legally, of course.

DR. LAURA: So get married already! What are you waiting for?

CALLER: For the courts to allow us.

DR. LAURA: So your wife is a man?

CALLER: He's not my wife; he's my partner. And yes, he's a man. What I was wondering was—

DR. LAURA: Drop him!

CALLER: No, that's not the issue. I was going to ask about—

DR. LAURA: Drop him and change! Get out of that relationship, get out of that phase you're going through, and get yourself a woman. Get out now. You're headed for nothing but trouble!

CALLER: Like I said, Dr. Laura, we're very happy together. All I wanted to know was—

DR. LAURA: You cannot be happy as a homosexual. You can't, and that's a fact. You might think you are happy, you might believe you are each pleasing the other, but you are not. You're not! You are a biological mistake, and you are living with another biological mistake. Two mistakes together. Two wrongs do not make a right! It's simple: Man was meant to provide pleasure for woman, and woman for man. Two men or two women...no. Absolutely not. That's nuts. Nuts!

CALLER: Dr. Laura—

DR. LAURA: It's craziness, I tell you. It's not right; it's just not natural. And I know all you people are going to start calling and writing and faxing and E-mailing the way you always do whenever I talk about homosexuals, and you know what? I don't want to hear it! Homosexuality is wrong! It's a perversion. It's perverse! It's loony. And it's not something that we need to sit here and argue about. Normal, intelligent Americans know what I'm talking about. They didn't choose to be gay, because they know it's wrong, and they don't want to talk about it or spend all kinds of time debating about it or even think about it. So that's my answer, and I know you don't like it, but you know what? I don't care. I don't care! Because I know that I'm right, and *you* know deep down in your heart that I'm right or else you wouldn't have called. It's not even worth arguing about. And I'm sorry, I apologize to my listeners, that they had to listen to this kind of drivel once more instead of hearing about real people with real problems they can relate to. So let's get back to the phones—

CALLER: Dr. Laura, wait—

Click

CALLER: Hi, Laurie. You'll never guess who this is.

DR. LAURA: You know, the voice sounds familiar. But come on, I don't have time for games. You're going to have to help me out here.

CALLER: OK, Laurie, I'll give you a hint. Third grade Brownies...sixth grade Campfire Girls...11th grade double-dating for the junior-senior prom....

DR. LAURA: Allison! Allison who I grew up with! Allison my long-lost best friend! Well, hello, and thanks for calling the *Dr. Laura Show*! What a wonderful surprise!

CALLER: It's been a long time.

DR. LAURA: Too long!

CALLER: And you know, I've been meaning to call for a long time.

DR. LAURA: You should have!

CALLER: I know, I know, I should have. I was so excited when you first came on the air. "Dr. Laura!" I told all the girls at my spinning class. "I know her! I grew up with her! She was my best friend all through school!"

DR. LAURA: I'll bet you have a great group of friends—and a family?

CALLER: Oh yes, I'll get to that in a sec. So I always meant to call because your advice was so good—so right-on. "That Laurie!" I said to myself. "She's so smart!" And you always were too, you know. You give everyone just the right advice, like you always did during Dodie's slumber parties.

DR. LAURA: Ha!

CALLER: So yeah, I was meaning to call you. And then... well, I don't know how to say this, Laurie, but, I don't know, a couple of things you've been saying lately, they just don't sound right to me. They don't sound like Laurie.

DR. LAURA: Don't sound right? What do you mean, Allie?

CALLER: Well, take what you're saying about gay people. It...some of it just is wrong, Laurie. You're not telling people the truth, and it hurts when I hear it, to think of some young boy or girl out there hearing Dr. Laura saying something, and thinking it's true, and—

DR. LAURA: Whoa, whoa! Hold your horses, Allison. What I say about homosexuals *is* the truth. Now let me ask you this, woman to woman, old friend to old friend: Is there something I should know about *you*?

CALLER: Not about me, no. I was married—to a man, don't worry—and I've got a wonderful son. He's—

DR. LAURA: Wow, you had me going there for a second! Because I do remember that junior-senior prom, and I didn't want to say anything before, but, well, let's just say, a lot of what I've learned came from watching you and Guy operate in the backseat!

CALLER: Don't remind me about that two-timing rat, please! But no, what I wanted to say—

DR. LAURA: So you're not homosexual. And you didn't marry one either, did you—ha, ha. Um—did you? Is that why you're no longer married?!

CALLER: Nope. But I—

DR. LAURA: Whew! But yet you called me up just to tell me I was wrong about the homosexuals? I'm sorry, Allie, but this just does not compute. I just don't get it. Can you explain this to me like I'm a 6-year-old: How did you get to be such an expert on the homosexual community? How do you know I'm wrong and you're right? And when you get right down to it, who really cares?

CALLER: Well, all I know is, they don't choose to be gay. I didn't choose to be straight, and they don't choose to be gay. They don't choose to be mocked, or laughed at, or wedgied in gym class, or thrown out of the house by their father when they come out of the closet after years of lies and deceit and torment. And they don't choose to be smacked over the head with a two-by-four, or have the windows of their home shot out, or strung up on a fence post and left to die.

DR. LAURA: I agree. No one deserves to have that happen to them. That's going a bit too far. But I also think—

CALLER: No, Laurie, I don't want to hear what you think. I want you to hear what *I* think. What I *know.* I want you to hear about my life—my life as the mother of a gay son.

DR. LAURA: The mother of a gay son! Allie, I'm so sorry.

CALLER: You are?

DR. LAURA: Yes!

CALLER: You're sorry for all the things you've said on the air, and written in the paper, and your books?

DR. LAURA: No! No! That's not what I meant. I'm sorry you have a homosexual son. That must be so very, very difficult for you.

CALLER: No! It's not! It's wonderful! I love him! He's my son—he's a great son, how could I *not* love him? I want to tell you about him. I want to talk about him—him and his partner. I want you to know him—*really* know him—so when you talk or write to millions of people about gays and lesbians you'll know what you're talking about.

DR. LAURA: Allison, I would not do this for just anyone. You know how I feel about homosexuals. But you also know how I feel about you. So yes, I would like to talk to you about your son. But we can't do it on the air. I must get to another caller. But someday soon, let's talk. I want to hear about your life as the mother of a gay son—and I do think it must be very, very difficult, no matter what you say. And then—only because you are such an old friend, you understand—maybe, one day, perhaps I could meet your son.

CALLER: Laurie, you already have.

DR. LAURA: Ha! I don't think so. Allie, hon, how on earth would I have met your son?

CALLER: He called just before me.

Who Gives a Toot?
A Speech by George W. Bush

Today, I am asking every gay man, lesbian, bisexual, and transgendered person in America for your vote for president of the United States. To the casual observer it may not seem as if I am on your side. But believe me, I am.

I have said many times, in many parts of this great nation, that I am a "compassionate conservative." And even though I have done my utmost to avoid weighing in on gay issues, I assure you, my compassionate side extends to you and your people.

I just have my own way of showing it.

For example, when I was asked about Texas legislation that would prohibit gay people from adopting children or serving as foster parents, I said, "I believe children ought to be adopted in families with a woman and a man who are married."

Critics claimed that was not a compassionate response. How wrong they were! In fact, it showed tremendous compassion for the children. Lord knows how much teasing and torment the child of a gay or lesbian couple might endure. Such youngsters might, through no fault of their own, be ostracized on the school bus, harassed on the playground, perhaps even marginalized by teachers and administrators. No child should ever have to put up with such indignities. So that stand was a way for me to proclaim compassion for a number of young Texans who, despite living in perhaps the first loving homes of their lives, might nonetheless face ridicule from peers and adults. As you can see, compassion oozes from every one of my conservative pores.

I have been criticized for the fact that at least six gay Texans have been brutally murdered since my election as governor, yet I have never commented publicly about those crimes. Once again, my compassion was working overtime. How hard it must be for the families of those victims to hear media reports that a loved one was not only dead, but gay. Imagine their grief as they listened to the news on television or read it in the newspaper. How insensitive it would be for me to add to such pain by making official statements denouncing the killings. So, compassionately, I kept my mouth shut.

Speaking of hate crimes, I took many hits for my opposition to the James Byrd Jr. Hate Crimes Act, a state bill that would have increased penalties for crimes motivated by bias based on a victim's race, ethnicity, gender, disability, religion, or sexual preference. "All crime is hate crime," I stated in the middle of the fervent debate.

Whether a black man is dragged to his death behind a pickup truck, a gay man is pistol-whipped and left on a fence post to die, a wealthy suburban family has its Range Rover stolen, or a john loses the services of his favorite prostitute after her arrest—every crime is a hate crime, and we all become victims.

Contrary to what my critics allege, my stands in favor of gay and lesbian people are strong indeed. In the summer of 1998, for example, Texas Republican officials prohibited the Log Cabin Republicans from setting up a booth at the state convention. They said their party did not allow booths for "pedophiles, transvestites, or cross-dressers."

And as soon as a Texas Republican spokesman compared the Log Cabin Republicans to the KKK, I spoke out strongly against "name-calling." After all, there is no need to denigrate a fine organization like the Klan.

I also opposed repeal of Texas's anti-sodomy law, even though it is archaic and biased against homosexuals. I read somewhere that butt sex leads directly to AIDS and thought keeping the law on the books might save a few homo lives. Compassion: That's my middle name.

It is also true that I have, at times, partied like a rich, white frat boy. But it was only so I could empathize with gay men—a group well-known for illicit drug use and wild orgies. Heck, what's a few lines in the service of compassion?

So, as you can see, I'm not antigay at all. I'm just misunderstood. And now that you understand that, I'm sure you'll turn out in droves to vote for me.

Thank you for your time. I'd take questions, but I really need to sneak out and powder my nose.

Scouts' Honor

Good afternoon, boys. Welcome to Boy Scout Camp. Before we begin, and to help ensure the most pleasant camping experience possible, I'd like to remind you that the Boy Scouts of America do not discriminate. It does not matter whether you are a Tenderfoot or Eagle Scout, a Scoutmaster or administrator, 12 years old or 72. If you are gay, you are out. We do not want you as a member of our organization.

Boy Scouts are, according to the 12 principles of Scout Law, trustworthy, loyal, helpful, friendly, courteous, kind, obedient, cheerful, thrifty, brave, clean, and reverent. The fact that the majority of gay men and boys could be described in similar terms is merely a cruel twist of fate. Boy Scouts are not gay!

The fact that our founder, Lord Baden-Powell, is rumored to have avoided women and to have carried on a long-term "friendship" with a fellow officer is immaterial. Boy Scouts are not gay!

The fact that many gay men fondly remember Boy Scout Camp as the place of their first same-sex sexual experience is nothing more than evidence of the depraved lunacy of homosexuals. Every sane person knows that boys don't do that. Well...not with each other. Well...not at Boy Scout Camp. Definitely not at Boy Scout Camp.

Just listen to the Boy Scout Oath:

"On my honor I will do my best
To do my duty to God and my country and to obey the Scout Law;
To help other people at all times;
To keep myself physically strong, mentally awake, and morally straight."

Did you catch those last two words? Morally straight. Straight! As in, not gay. Boy Scouts are not gay!

Now, which of you adorable little heterosexuals wants to sleep in my tent tonight?

The Grand Duchy
An Open Letter From the People of Luxembourg to the Citizens of the United States

All we wanted was an ambassador. We never meant to cause any trouble. Truly, that is not our style.

The Grand Duchy of Luxembourg is a tiny land. We are smaller than your tiniest state, Rhode Island, and our population is less than that of your least populous one, Wyoming. We have been overrun more than 20 times in five centuries by the likes of Philip the Good of Burgundy, the Hapsburgs, Spain, the Netherlands, and all three of our neighbors (France, Germany, and Belgium). We have survived all that, including two world wars; it's not as if we were looking for a hardliner to come in and protect us.

So we would be the first to admit that when President Clinton set about finding us an ambassador, it probably was not the most pressing decision of his presidency. In October 1997 he nominated James C. Hormel. He was supremely qualified to be ambassador: a 64-year-old man from San Francisco (like Luxembourg, an important banking center) with bundles of money and a head full of diplomatic-looking white hair. As heir to the Hormel meatpacking fortune, he knew his way around boardrooms and was intimately connected with the political party in power. What more could a tiny duchy want? It's not as if he were being appointed ambassador to someplace important like Russia or China. We have never stolen nuclear secrets and could not start World War III if our lives depended on it.

The news of Mr. Hormel's nomination thrilled us. The last time we welcomed such a high-powered American ambassador was half a century ago, when President Truman sent us Perle Mesta, the legendary Washington hostess. We have not seen such lavish parties since, and hoped that, since he is a gay man, Mr. Hormel might be an excellent cook or, failing that, would at least know some excellent caterers.

Knowing more about the United States than the United States knows about Luxembourg, we were not surprised when opposition arose to Mr. Hormel. After all, his lifestyle is anathema to many Republicans: He sat on the board of his local chamber of commerce; he spent his free hours donating, and helping raise, tens of millions of dollars for such causes as the Holocaust Museum, breast cancer and AIDS research, and San

Francisco's symphony, public library, and ballet. We certainly looked forward to the arrival of the philanthropic Mr. Hormel. Every duchy needs a symphony and ballet.

Other lines in his resume also sent the Republicans up a wall, as you Americans say. He served the United States through his appointment to the U.N. General Assembly in 1996 and was a delegate to the Human Rights Commission in Geneva. When last we looked, the United Nations survived, and Switzerland too still stands. If we had something to hide, we would surely be up in arms over his U.N. service, but as duchies go, we are pretty clean. We have never been accused of any human rights abuses. All our garment workers are of legal age and are paid fair wages. Well, they would be if we had any garment factories, that's for sure.

In short, Mr. Hormel seems eminently qualified for this post. Many ambassadors are not. When Jimmy Carter sent Richard Kneip to Singapore, the former South Dakota governor asked his staff, "Did you say there are two separate Koreas? How come?" George Bush appointed former Republican senator Chic Hecht of Nevada as ambassador to the Bahamas. Senator Hecht noted that he was qualified because of his enthusiasm for gambling and golf. Bush also sent Joy Silverman to Barbados even though she never went to college or held a job. Her main qualification was her husband, who gave $180,000 to the Republican Party in 1988. Ronald Reagan, a true Republican hero, named Theodore Maino as ambassador to Kenya. Mr. Maino said he looked forward to big-game hunting. Unfortunately, that is banned in Kenya.

Sen. Trent Lott worried that, because our duchy is 98% Catholic, we might not accept a gay man as ambassador. He thought we would be offended by Mr. Hormel's links to the Sisters of Perpetual Indulgence, a San Francisco troupe of drag queens who dress as nuns. (It turns out Mr. Hormel's "support" for the Sisters consisted of appearing at the same 500,000-person parade as they.) Frankly, we think drag queens imitating nuns is a marvelous idea. We may be just a duchy, but that doesn't mean we do not have a sense of humor.

Speaking of San Francisco, perhaps the Republican opponents of Mr. Hormel do not know that years ago our duchy outlawed discrimination against gay people—just like Mr. Hormel's hometown and unlike the U.S. government. We find it intriguing that the same senators who say their country does not need legislation to protect gay people discriminated against Mr. Hormel because he is gay. As for us, we are far more interested in the fact that he is chairman of an investment company. That turns Luxembourgers on the most. We are into finance, not fetish.

Though the White House said Mr. Hormel had the support of 60 senators and the Republican-controlled Foreign Relations Committee approved his nomination 16-2, Senator Lott, the majority leader, flatly refused to let the nomination come to the floor.

Eventually President Clinton appointed Mr. Hormel as ambassador to Luxembourg in June 1999 during a congressional recess. Senator Lott, we are aware, called Mr. Clinton's move "a subversion of the confirmation process," conveniently forgetting that in 6½ years President Clinton made 57 recess appointments, while President Bush made 78 in four years, and President Reagan 239 in eight.

It seems clear to us that President Clinton would not have had to make a recess appointment if Senator Lott had agreed to let the original nomination be brought to the floor of the Senate in 1977. Please correct us if we are wrong on that one.

We are sorry Mr. Hormel had to slip in through the proverbial "back door." However, we welcome him with open arms as well as with a friendly kiss on each cheek. That is the Grand Duchy of Luxembourg way.

Lesbians for Liberty: Covert Operations Report

Ladies: As expected, the WNBA has responded to our recent unfurling in support of the New York Liberty franchise of a "Lesbians for Liberty" banner at Madison Square Garden by instituting a blanket ban on all things lesbian during WNBA telecasts.

The following is an internal WNBA memo obtained by one of our many spies.

* * *

TO: Producers, directors, on-air talent, camera operators, sound technicians, and all others connected with WNBA (Women's National Basketball Association) telecasts
FROM: Advertising department
RE: WNBA game telecasts

First, we wish to congratulate all of you on an outstanding achievement. The WNBA is off to a strong start ratings-wise. If current growth continues, the WNBA may one day take its rightful place alongside the men's league as a major sports marketing vehicle. We would then be in excellent position to market the WNBA to advertisers using such time-honored audience-grabbing sales points as trash-talking, bruising physical confrontations, players wearing outrageous hairdos, and body mutilation.

Until that time, however, we must nurture our fledgling league by protecting its fragile image. We must remain vigilant of our product. Perception is reality, and we should never let fans perceive that the *L* word has been added to the letters "WNBA."

It is no secret that lesbians have long been attracted to women's sports. In fact, rumor has it that several lesbians are among the WNBA's player ranks. Furthermore, many teams are attracting zealous groups of lesbian fans. The alleged lesbians are some of our best players and certainly our most loyal fans, and Legal has advised us that declaring the WNBA a "lesbian-free zone" is neither feasible nor constitutional. So we're stuck with them.

But that does not mean we can't sweep them under the rug. To that end, we insist that the following standards be adhered to at all times during WNBA broadcasts:

CROWD SHOTS must include men. Avoid clusters of females;

any time two women are shown, they must always be separated by at least one male. Never show two women with a baby. (Mothers and fathers sharing an infant are, of course, a coveted shot.) When players' husbands are shown, the men must quickly be identified as such via both a screen crawl and the sportscaster's own words. Boyfriends should be identified only by the sportscaster.

COACHES must be televised in as feminine a manner as possible. Shots to look for include coaches wearing skirts or high-heeled shoes. Pink is an excellent color. Shots to avoid include coaches wearing pants or sensible shoes. Rainbow anything—clothing, jewelry, hair—is to be avoided.

PLAYERS: Wedding rings make nice TV shots; so do crucifixes and/or other religious symbols. If a player is shown looking into the stands, announcers should make reference to the husband or boyfriend being sought. Televised postgame interviews should not begin until a player is surrounded by her children; multiple offspring are preferable to single boys or girls. Under no circumstances are nonplaying women to be allowed to wander into the interview area. NO EXCEPTIONS!

BANNERS AND SIGNS: Avoid training cameras on banners, signs, posters, or other visual aids that might, whether intentional or otherwise, be perceived as promoting lesbianism. For example, a contingent of Madison Square Garden fans raised a "Lesbians for Liberty" banner in favor of the New York home team. Although the WNBA Web site features an entire section urging fans to make original signs, security guards ordered the lesbians to remove their banner on the grounds that Madison Square Garden policy restricts signs because they block other people's views. We were fortunate that that problem was handled without league or network involvement. However, inadvertent shots of similar signs might encourage copycats, and arenas could be awash with such suggestive signs.

NOTE: It has been brought to our attention that New York Liberty lesbian fans have begun wearing T-shirts and buttons, with such messages as "Madison Queer Garden" and "Another Lesbian for Liberty." The prohibition against televising banners and signs extends to T-shirts, buttons, and any other message-bearing apparel.

STORY LINES should, whenever possible, refer to players' off-court activities, provided those activities involve such traditionally female hobbies as gardening, child-rearing, or helping one's husband around the house. Do not mention such pastimes as motorcycle riding, home improvement, or attending the Dinah Shore golf tournament.

ADVERTISING sales efforts should concentrate on perfume, cosmetics, lingerie, feminine hygiene, hair care, handbags, and movies starring Mel Gibson, Brad Pitt, or any of the Baldwins. Do not sell advertising time to Snap-On tools, Home Depot, Olivia cruises, or recording companies affiliated with k.d. lang, Melissa Etheridge, Janis Ian, or the Indigo Girls.

Thank you in advance for your cooperation.

* * *

In response, Lesbians for Liberty suggest womyn who love the WNBA and its many players and fans wear buttons and/or T-shirts with slogans such as "Dykes Take It to the Hole!" We also suggest chanting "We're here, we're queer, and we know how to score!" during all game action. Rest your throats at halftime and during commercial breaks. You'll need them later.

Don't Ask...

BARBARA WALTERS: Mr. President, welcome. As you end your two terms in office, I appreciate your willingness to talk about some of the highlights and low points of the past eight years. Can we begin with one of your first controversies, "Don't ask, don't tell"?

PRESIDENT CLINTON: Barbara, it's a pleasure to be here. Before I begin, let me say one thing. The end of my eight years in office marks the end of a long journey for me. It is a journey that began in a place called Hope. The journey continued through places called Yale and Oxford, and on through places called Little Rock and Whitewater. It has taken me to my favorite place of all, the Oval Office and its nearby nooks and crannies.

On my journey I have wanted to do the right thing, but it has been hard. Just as I lust for certain visceral things—Big Macs, pizzas, interns with big hair—I have an intangible desire to satisfy every American. Liberal Democrats, conservative Republicans, pig farmers, venture capitalists, small-business owners, Hollywood titans, gay activists, and even bigots. For some reason I feel the need to please them all. Naturally, along the way some people have gotten screwed. I apologize. I have caused pain for many Americans. I feel your pain.

Some of those Americans who have felt pain are my lesbian, gay, bisexual, and transgendered friends. I assure you, my heart was in the right place. Unfortunately, a very important other part of my body—my head—was not.

First, let me mention the things I have done on behalf of the lesbian, gay, bisexual, and transgender community.

I supported ENDA—the Employment Non-Discrimination Act. Now, I know I didn't actually get down in the trenches and fight for it the way the gay community would have liked, but I did that with health care, and look where it got me.

I mentioned the word "gay" in my 1996 Democratic national convention acceptance speech. I know I tend to talk too long and try to say too much, but including gay people in that speech meant a lot to me. And I'm sure it jolted many listeners out of their dozing-off state.

During one of my State of the Union messages I spoke about the importance of gay rights. Now, I'm no Ronald Reagan at these things—he would have pointed out some little-known gay hero at exactly that moment, bringing tears to even Jesse Helms's eyes—but the point is, he never would have said such a thing in the first place. Even though he was an actor—and was friends with Rock Hudson, for crying out loud—Ronald Reagan never mentioned gay rights in his State of the Union speeches. I did.

Speaking of speaking, I hope you remember the appearance I made at the Human Rights Campaign dinner. Obviously, it's hard to keep me away from any kind of fund-raiser—even one that is not my own—but this was another historic moment. No sitting president had ever addressed a gay group. And the ovation I got just for walking in! It was truly memorable. I could have stood up, blown on my sax, sat down, and they would have been happy. But no, I delivered a speech, I stopped to kiss Ellen DeGeneres and Anne Heche—I drew the line at kissing Barney Frank, not that there's anything wrong with that, you understand—and it was a wonderful night. Nothing like hanging out with gay people to keep your mind off Monica Lewinsky!

I also nominated Jim Hormel as ambassador to Luxembourg—and stuck with him. And then, in a masterstroke—a congressional recess!—I rammed his appointment through.

Jim Hormel was not the only gay person I appointed to a high position. There was Roberta Achtenberg, Virginia Apuzzo, Bob Hattoy, Richard Socarides, Sean Maloney, and a couple of closeted cabinet members, although I swore I wouldn't say anything about their sexuality unless they wanted me to, and that's one of the few promises I'm willing to keep. I would have given my old friend David Mixner a good job too, except we had a falling-out and he didn't speak to me for a while. He's still a great guy, though, and he's more than welcome to come around and help me raise money the next time I need it.

I also issued an official proclamation recognizing June as Gay and Lesbian Pride Month and signed an executive order prohibiting discrimination in the federal civilian workforce based on sexual orientation. That's the kind of policy wonk stuff that really gets my blood racing. Did I enjoy sticking it to the Republicans and making sure that all this talk about "compassionate conservatism" is really so much baloney? You bet I did. But I still believe these were the right things to do.

Of course, that does not mean I'm in anyone's back pocket. I know the gay community has had their issues with me, just like everyone else in the country. I don't think there's a constituency in America I haven't ticked off or upset at one time or another, Barbara.

And the very first people I ticked off—it was within hours of taking office, actually—were lesbians and gays. That happened because of "don't ask, don't tell," and you know, looking back, that was probably the biggest boner of my whole presidency. Here I'd gone around the country soliciting gay and lesbian votes, asking for money and support from the gay community, which I got. But when push came to shove, I collapsed like a bad soufflé. And that's how the whole "don't ask, don't tell" policy came about.

The gay community got even more upset, and rightfully so, when I signed DOMA in the middle of the night. Afterward, of course, I ran campaign ads boasting about it. That was an incredibly weasely thing to do. But when you come right down to it, I'm a politician, and politicians can be weasels.

Lesbian and gays keep saying I stabbed them in the back. But who haven't I stabbed in the back? I've capitulated on welfare reform, immigration reform, health care, you name it. I've tried to be all things to all people, and every time I've failed. So I can see where lesbians and gays would have issues with me. Heck, everyone in America does. In my heart, though, I think most gays and lesbians know I'm on their side. Just think about all my fooling around: Single-handedly I showed America that it's not just gay people who are obsessed with sex, who get hummers and whatnot in the strangest places. After all my little flings, nobody can ever call gay sex "deviant" again. If that doesn't show where my sympathies lie, I don't know what does.

BARBARA WALTERS: That was a very long answer, Mr. President, to my question about "don't ask, don't tell." But the American people appreciate hearing your side of things. Now, unfortunately, time is running out.

PRESIDENT CLINTON: It's my pleasure, Barbara. And if I can say just one more thing: I think your hair looks wonderful done up like that. I mean it. It really, really looks great. Do you want to come back to the Oval Office and look at my edition of *Leaves of Grass*? It's by Walt Whitman. He was a gay man, you know.

Happy Mother's Day!

Dear Mothers Everywhere:

In May of 1999 the Center for Reclaiming America celebrated Mother's Day with a gift more meaningful than any card, bouquet of flowers, box of chocolates, or surprise breakfast in bed.

Together with 18 pro-family and religious organizations, we launched a unique television advertisement targeted especially at your mom. Our 60-second ad featured Frances Johnston of Newport News, Va. A mom, just like you, Frances gazed lovingly at the camera and said, "I love my son very much. I always have. Even when he told me he was using drugs and involved in homosexuality." Her motherly tone signaled a great big "but" waiting in the wings. "But," continued Frances, "just because you love your children doesn't mean you approve of everything they do. Sometimes they make bad choices. My son Michael found out the truth. He could walk away from homosexuality, but he found out too late. He has AIDS."

Frances pleaded, "If you love your children, love them enough to let them know the truth. There is hope for change, hope for the future."

The "truth," of course, was that, unlike leopards, homosexuals can change their spots. Homosexuals can become normal, straight people. What finer gift than this knowledge could any mother want?

Surprisingly, major network affiliates refused to air our advertisement. In retrospect, this might not be such a bad thing. You see, in the uproar that followed we realized we had not quite thought our actions through.

We did not stop to think that our slickly produced advertisement showing a mother in amazing turmoil over her son's homosexuality might have devastating effects on some of the most vulnerable members of society: gay youth. It also completely slipped our notice that equating homosexuality with AIDS is a wee bit out-of-date. Frankly, we were shocked—shocked!—to learn that heterosexual teenagers are now one of the highest risk groups for contracting HIV.

Furthermore, we had no idea that every respected mental health and medical organization has flatly rejected "ex-gay" ministries and reparative therapy. Needless to say, we've fired our fact checkers.

In conclusion, we, the mothers at the Center for Reclaiming America, would like to say that the intense reaction against our ads has helped us recognize that it is not our homosexual children that must be changed but our homophobic attitudes. We now understand that the motherhood we celebrate on Mother's Day—and the family values we cherish the rest of the year—are based on acceptance and unconditional love, not mean-spirited, underhanded television ads.

We apologize for our insensitivity to mothers, especially mothers of homosexuals. Honestly we do. We swear it on our mothers' graves.

The Gay Agenda

All right, OK. More than 30 years after Stonewall, a century after Oscar Wilde was sentenced to hard labor in prison, and several millennia after Greek men cavorted with their "special young friends," we admit it: There *is* a Gay Agenda.

And it's time to bring it out of the closet.

Those in the Right have always suspected the gay community of having an agenda, and they are indeed right. Here, in all its rainbow splendor, is The Gay Agenda.

* *We want special rights.* Absolutely true. We want the right to not be physically assaulted—even murdered—simply for existing. We want the right to say "I do" in a lawfully recognized marriage ceremony and, thus, the right to provide for our spouses through pensions, inheritances, and health insurance. We want the right to see our children following divorce from a legal spouse or a breakup with a same-gender partner. We want the right to serve in the armed forces. We want the right to live the same life as straight Americans. We're not saying we actually want to live that life; we just want to know it's possible.
* *We want to celebrate our past, present, and future at gay pride events.* No one questions the existence of a St. Patrick's Day parade or Cinco de Mayo. So why the fuss over gay pride? We realize that dykes on bikes and men wearing leather aren't for everyone, but they're just as vital a part of our queer community as gay teachers, choirs, police officers, and bowling clubs. And are they really any more offensive than a bunch of drunken Irishmen?
* *We want to live in suburban towns and on rural farms, not just selected areas of large cities.* We plan to blend in—joining the Rotary and PTA, working at the county fair and alongside our neighbors. We plan to lead solid, civic-oriented lives. Then we plan to have a gay pride parade. Do you hear us, Oregon? We're coming. You're next.
* *We want to protect the most vulnerable members of our community: gay youth.* We want the world to know that gay teenagers face such overpowering social, family, academic, and emotional pressures that they attempt (and succeed at) suicide in numbers far greater than their straight peers. We want school administrators to provide safe educational environments for all students regardless of their sexual orientation. We want a gay-straight alliance in every school district in America. And we want people to know that gay-straight alliances are vehicles for overcoming bigotry, not sex clubs.
* *We want the federal government to extend its prohibitions against discrimination on the basis of race, religion, gender, national origin, age, and disability to include sexual orientation.* We know our legislators are busy writing tax codes that make rich campaign contributors even richer, but adding two little words—*sexual orientation*—to a set of laws that already exist can't be that hard.
* *We want the right to love and adopt children.* For some of us, that means bearing legal responsibility for the biological children of our lovers. For others, it means helping care for our own biological children. For still others, it means fostering and/or adopting babies, toddlers, even teenagers no one else wants. This part of the Gay Agenda has been deemed threatening by a number of American courts at various levels. Judges, it seems, would rather award custody of a child to a murderer than a lesbian or to a state agency instead of a gay man. We don't understand this. Children need love, and we have love to spare.
* *We want the government to repeal laws that discriminate against gays and lesbians, such as*

sodomy statutes. In nearly half of America's states those laws remain on the books. They are used only occasionally, to be sure—and some states have not had a prosecution in years. But we still want these laws repealed, because any kind of antigay prejudice rankles us. We're funny that way.

* We *want to recruit*. That's right: We want to make sure every gay man, lesbian, bisexual, and transgendered person feels comfortable in the gay community. We want their friends and relatives to feel part of us too. We know we can't make someone gay any more than we can make ourselves straight, but we *can* make someone who is already gay more self-confident and comfortable with that identity.

* We *want a "gay lifestyle."* The media constantly refers to the "gay lifestyle," so we suppose such a thing must exist. And we want it. It sounds fabulous. So whichever demented hetero it is that's hoarding the gay lifestyle, please fork it over. It's ours. It's even got our name on it.

* We *want the right to think about sex*. Straight people think about sex all the time. They also talk about it, joke about it, and show it on television and movies and in advertisements. Yet every time gay people raise the topic, we are accused by straight people of "shoving it down their throats." (How's *that* for a metaphor!) Well, tit for tat. You've shoved *your* sex down *our* throats for centuries, and we're tired of it. It's our turn to top.

* We *want to promote "family values."* This is a particularly difficult element of the Agenda to explain, especially to the radical right. For the life of us, we cannot understand why "the family" is an institution the far right feels is threatened by homosexuality. It seems pretty obvious to us that extending the concept of "family" to gays and lesbians won't cause straight families to instantly, tragically fall apart.

* We *want the world to understand that being gay is not a choice*. We did not choose to be gay any more than a straight person chooses to be straight. And we are tired of idiots who know nothing about us telling people otherwise.

* We *want religious organizations to stick to their traditional agendas: providing spiritual guidance to those who seek it and charity to those who need it*. We want conservative religious leaders to stop using us as a way of furthering their own ambitions. We are people, not a fund-raising ploy.

That is the Gay Agenda. It is not so radical, is it? However, we are sorry for having tried to impose it on an unwilling society. We apologize for any convenience it may have caused. We'll go quietly now, back from where we came. If for any reason you want us, we'll be where we always were: in your towns, your homes, and your families.

Off My Rocker

Public Announcement by John Rocker at Shea Stadium

Before I begin, just a reminder [*points to scoreboard television screen*]. My remarks are being signed for the hearing-impaired. It's the least I can do for fans less fortunate than I.

Let me start by apologizing for my recent remarks regarding New York City and its wonderfully diverse population. I owe a special apology to all riders of the number 7 subway line. I've never taken it myself, because major league ballplayers get chauffeured everywhere. But I heard about it at my hotel from a maid who rode it to watch me play. I appreciate her support. She said she spent $20 on a ticket, $9.50 for a hot dog and soda, and $22 for souvenirs. At least she didn't have to pay for parking.

I apologize to people with purple hair. My father always told me what's inside a person's head is more important than what's on it, but baseball players don't usually think much beyond spitters, sliders, and how to spend our multimillion-dollar salaries.

I apologize to everyone I offended with my "queers with AIDS" crack too. I had a gay teammate once and he was OK, after I realized he wasn't going to hit on me in the shower. In fact, when I asked him why not, he said I wasn't good-looking enough. I'm no Calvin Klein model, but that surprised me. I guess there's no accounting for taste.

I apologize too to all the 20-year-old moms with four kids. I know a few guys in baseball who are 20 and also have four kids. The difference is, they're not raising them themselves. In fact, most of those guys don't even know where their four kids live.

Finally, I want to apologize to two more groups I offended: people who don't speak English and dudes who just got out of jail. That was really dumb. Without those guys I wouldn't have a league to play in.

Time for Truth

In our May 17, 1999, issue, we reported on the allegations by longtime activist, noted playwright, and professional agitator Larry Kramer that Abraham Lincoln—the much revered 16th president of the United States—was a closeted homosexual. We then moved a bit beyond Mr. Kramer's historical research into the sleeping arrangements of Mr. Lincoln and his special friend, Joshua Speer, running a sidebar that included several reasons "Honest Abe" might also have been known by the moniker "Dishonest Gaybe." Among our presumptions:

* He once abandoned Mary Todd at the altar.
* He liked the theater.
* He experimented with fashion (dressed all in black, wore a snazzy hat).

We apologize for not digging deeper in our earlier report. Further investigation by a team of *Time* special reporters reveals that Mr. Lincoln was hardly the sole gay man to occupy and, upon moving in, redecorate the White House. Astonishingly, every one of the 41 U.S. presidents has been a homosexual.

This revelation will surprise many historians, ordinary citizens, and curators of museums with exhibits dedicated to the "Dresses of America's First Ladies." The news has already stunned mathematicians, who argue that the percentage of gay presidents—now estimated at 100—is a statistical near-impossibility. Using the generally accepted figure that 10% of the population is gay, the number of homosexual presidents should be 4.1. However, when it comes to American presidents, statistical anomalies abound. For example, the percentage of female American presidents (0) falls far short of their representation among the population at large (51).

Time's special report contains a number of intriguing revelations. Some presidents were clearly "more gay" than others. However, all demonstrated at least one homosexual tendency. Listed below is a blow-by-blow description of Our Homosexual American Presidents.

George Washington (1789–97)
* Could not tell a lie; however, never was specifically asked "Sir, are you gay?"
* Wore false teeth made from expensive ivory that matched powdered wig.
* Married Martha Custis, wealthy widow.
* While crossing Delaware River in rowboat, stood up to strike pose.
* Had habit of sleeping in different taverns and inns each night.
* "Father of Our Country" had no children.
* While doctors bled him in vain attempt to save his life, worried about stains on designer linen.

John Adams (1797–1801)
* Nickname as vice president: "Bonny Johnny Adams."

Thomas Jefferson (1801–09).
* Turned back on organized religion: Advocated reading the Bible with "the same critical eye that one would cast on any book."
* Loved Paris.

* As president, spent $15 million for Louisiana Purchase, paving the way for creation of New Orleans's French Quarter.

James Madison (1809–17)
* Sickly, weak, and nervous youth; tried to appear tougher by engaging in rigorous exercise.
* Very shy with women—did not get married until 43. With wife Dolley, threw fabulous parties.

James Monroe (1817–25)
* Monroe Doctrine: In order to enforce it, U.S. had to rely on British semen. Oops, seamen.

John Quincy Adams (1825–29)
* In Paris, studied fencing, dance, music, and art; at Harvard, played flute.
* Hobbies: observing nature, domesticating wild plants, theater, fine wines (one night after dinner, correctly identified 11 of 14 Madeiras).

Andrew Jackson (1829–37)
* Enjoyed cockfights.
* First president to have nipple pierced (by bullet in duel, 1806).

Martin Van Buren (1837–41)
* According to Rep. Davy Crockett of Tennessee: "He is what the English call a dandy. When he enters the senate chamber in the morning, he struts and swaggers like a crow in the gutter. He is laced up in corsets, such as women in town wear, and, if possible, tighter than the best of them. It would be difficult to say, from his personal appearance, whether he was man or woman but for his large...whiskers."
* Opera buff.
* In presidential campaign of 1840, was candidate of "the silk-stocking set."

William Henry Harrison (1841)
* Often described as "urbane."
* Enjoyed doing his own marketing before breakfast, even as president.
* Loved to talk: For example, could not shut up during inauguration speech (lasted one hour, 40 minutes, a presidential record). Proved poor career move, as he delivered address in brisk March wind without hat, gloves, or overcoat; on way back to White House, got caught in a downpour, fell ill with "bilious pleurisy," died one month later.

John Tyler (1841–45)
* Played violin: Favorite tune was "Home Sweet Home."
* Raised canaries and greyhounds.
* Courted wife, Letitia, for five years; did not kiss her until a few weeks before the wedding—and then only on the hand.

James K. Polk (1845–49)
* Felt out of place in the rough-and-tumble atmosphere of frontier Tennessee: On surveying trips with father, preferred to stay close to camp and cook.
* Gave name to world-famous male hustler area, San Francisco's Polk Street.

Zachary Taylor (1849–50)
* Member of the Whig Party; however, seldom wore one, although often searched for something to match his pearls.

Millard Fillmore (1850–53)
* Named "Millard Fillmore."

* Meticulous dresser.
* Compromise of 1850 admitted California, and therefore San Francisco, into union.

Franklin Pierce (1853–57)
* Taught elementary school.
* Kansas-Nebraska Act of 1854 promoted settlement of Kansas Territory; less than century later, film classic *The Wizard of Oz* set there.

James Buchanan (1857–61)
* Had strong, deep, and flagrant 23-year friendship with William Rufus De Vane King, vice president under Franklin Pierce, a man known for "fastidious habits."
* Buchanan was only unmarried president; King was only unmarried vice president.
* Andrew Jackson called King "Miss Nancy." Others called him "Buchanan's better half" and "Aunt Fancy." James K. Polk's law partner called him "Mrs. James Buchanan" and frequently referred to "Buchanan and his wife."
* When King was appointed minister to France, he wrote Buchanan: "I am selfish enough to hope you will not be able to procure an associate who will cause you to feel no regret at our separation."
* Buchanan and King were roommates in Washington.

Abraham Lincoln (1861–65)
* Would have been on debate team if he had gone to school.
* Like predecessor Buchanan, had a "roommate" for whom he showed deep affection. Affection was mutual—Joshua Speer wrote: "He often kisses me when I tease him, often to shut me up. He would grab me up by his long arms and hug and hug. Yes, our Abe is like a schoolgirl."
* Married certifiably crazy woman, Mary Todd.
* Strong feelings for persecuted minorities.
* Observed, "You can fool some of the people all of the time, and all of the people some of the time, but you can't fool all of the people all of the time."

Andrew Johnson (1865–69)
* Enjoyed puttering in vegetable garden; also liked the circus.
* Impeached by Congress that intensely disliked him—and *not* for having sex with a female intern.

Ulysses S. Grant (1869–77)
* Named "Ulysses."
* According to biographer W.E. Woodward, "Young Grant had a girl's primness of manner and modesty of conduct. There was a broad streak of the feminine in his personality. He was almost half woman, but this strain was buried in the depths of his soul; it never came to the surface except indirectly, and he was probably not aware of it himself."
* At West Point, was elected president of the Dialectic (Literary) Society.
* Engaged for four years to Julia Dent; during that time they saw each other only once.

Rutherford B. Hayes (1877–81)
* As a young man, thought he was crazy.
* Grew up and realized he was not.

James A. Garfield (1881)
* Severely depressed as a young adult; after being elected president, had nightmares of being naked and lost.
* Doted on at home by mother and siblings, teased by peers.
* Clumsy: Several times gashed self with ax, often fell down doing chores.

* Considered taking up the ministry; went into teaching instead.
* Enjoyed Jane Austen novels.
* Killed by assassin while strolling arm in arm with Secretary of State James G. Blaine through the waiting room of Washington railroad station.

Chester A. Arthur (1881–85)
* Fastidious dresser, nicknamed "Elegant Arthur"; had 80 pairs of pants, changed clothes several times a day.
* Said: "I may be president of the United States, but my private life is nobody's damned business."

Grover Cleveland (1885–89; 1893–97)
* Minister's son.
* "Went both ways": Only president elected to two non-successive terms.

Benjamin Harrison (1889–93)
* Came both before and after Grover Cleveland.

William McKinley (1897–1901)
* Refused to be photographed unless impeccably groomed; enjoyed wearing red carnations.
* Hobbies: Opera and theater.
* Second president to have nipple pierced (by bullet, during successful assassination attempt, 1901).

Theodore Roosevelt (1901–09)
* Spindly, pale, asthmatic as boy; through rigorous workouts, transformed self into macho man.
* Enjoyed wrestling.
* Made "meat inspection" an important issue.
* Spoke softly.
* Carried "big stick."

William Howard Taft (1909–13)
* Liked musical comedies.

Woodrow Wilson (1913–21)
* Nicknamed "Woody."
* Sang tenor in glee club.

Warren G. Harding (1921–23)
* Mother called him "Winnie."
* In election of 1920, beat Cox.

Calvin Coolidge (1923–29)
* Hobby: Window-shopping.
* Was mayor of Northampton, Mass.

Herbert Hoover (1929–33)
* Enduring legacy: depression.

Franklin D. Roosevelt (1933–45)
* Mama's boy: Wore dresses until he was 5, kilts until he was 8.
* At Groton (private boys school), enjoyed dance lessons, sang soprano in the choir, managed baseball team, was dormitory prefect.

* Used elegant cigarette holder.
* Married a lesbian.

Harry S. Truman (1945–53)
* As child, wore thick, expensive glasses, and was under strict orders not to roughhouse or play contact sports. Said of self: "To tell the truth, I was kind of a sissy. If there was any danger of getting into a fight, I always ran."
* Before presidency, worked in men's clothing industry.

Dwight D. Eisenhower (1953–61)
* Hobbies: bridge and canasta.
* Ended Korean War; sent Klinger home.

John F. Kennedy (1961–63)
* Too good-looking to be straight.
* Domineering mother.
* In 1953, was subject of *Saturday Evening Post* story: "Jack Kennedy—The Senate's Gay Young Bachelor."

Lyndon B. Johnson (1963–69)
* Nickname: "El B.J."

Richard M. Nixon (1969–74)
* One word: Dick.

Gerald R. Ford (1974–77)
* Played football but kept falling down.
* Worked as male model.

Jimmy Carter (1977–81)
* Battled killer rabbit to a draw.

Ronald Reagan (1981–89)
* Activities in college: swim team, debate team, basketball cheerleader, president of student council, feature editor of yearbook, reporter for student newspaper.
* Often fabricated tales about his life.
* Movie actor.

George Bush (1989–93)
* Nickname: Poppy.
* Married white-haired lady who looked like his mother.
* Once said "read my lips"; later amended it to "watch my hips."
* Obsessed with "Sodom" Hussein.

Bill Clinton (1993–2001)
* Discussed underwear preference on national television.
* Continually managed to get "caught" with women in "compromising" situations.
* Cigars.

Jiminy Cricket!

To our valued guests:

Today is unofficially Gay Day. Disney has no official connection with either Gay Day or the equally unofficial Protest Day that follows in its wake. We neither condemn nor condone any group that wishes to attend en masse (gays and lesbians pour in by the tens of thousands) or en few (the last Protest Day garnered less than a dozen sign-wielding homophobic zealots). We believe all citizens, regardless of race, religion, gender, ethnic background, age, physical ability, sexual orientation, or outdated fear of anyone different, should be able to enjoy Uncle Walt's fantasy world. We believe *every* human being has the God-given right to wear Hawaiian shirts, pay high prices for bad food, stand in long lines for short rides, and listen to corny jokes from low-paid employees we grandly call "cast members."

Having said that, we must admit we like our Gay Day patrons more than our Protest Day patrons. They dress better, have more fun, and purchase more Disney products throughout the year. We recognize, however, that some guests feel uncomfortable during Gay Day. If you are one of those individuals, we recommend that you avoid the following sites and attractions:

* *Aladdin.* Youngsters learn that rubbing something can bring exquisite pleasure.
* *All-American Family Barbecue.* A country hoedown with Mickey and Minnie Mouse, Goofy, and Chip and Dale. Chip and Dale are famous male strippers.
* *Animal Kingdom.* Virtually every species of animal in the world exhibits some form of same-gender behavior. On "Gay Day," hand-holding humans join in the fun.
* *Carousel of Progress.* Located in Tomorrowland, this attraction is famous for its theme song, "There's a Great Big Beautiful Tomorrow." Guests who are worried about what tomorrow might bring should stay away.
* *Country Bear Jamboree.* "Bear" is gay slang for large, hairy men. In past years gay guests have become smitten with Brer Bear, whose animatronic butt is apparently quite cute.
* *Dapper Dans.* Four guys sing show tunes on Main Street U.S.A.
* *Dumbo the flying elephant.* With all those hot guys walking around, there's no telling how excited Dumbo could get. Look out below!
* *Ellen's Energy Ride.* Shows Ellen DeGeneres, a known lesbian, interacting positively with Bill Nye the Science Guy.
* *Enchanted Tiki Birds.* Singing birds and plants, with The Lion King's Zazu as host. Word on the street is he's "family" (and we don't mean Dad, Mom, and 2.2 kids).
* *Fantasyland.* Anything can happen once you allow your fantasies to run wild. Stay away!
* *Fountain at Innoventions Plaza:* Two words: water ballet.
* *It's a Small World.* Teaches tolerance for others.
* *Jungle "cruise."* You'll particularly want to avoid the boat named "Scarlet Flamingo."
* *"Making of Life."* Sensitive film includes footage of a developing fetus. Baby may turn out to be gay.
* *Mickey's Toontown.* Mickey welcomes guests into his "country house"; visit includes gardens out back.
* *Minnie's House.* Minnie lives near Mickey; their relationship is unclear. At Disney World, Minnie is "the cartoon Martha Stewart," and during Gay Day her house will be filled with

thousands of gay men checking out the kitchen and furnishings.
* *Pirates of the Caribbean.* Swarthy men on a boat with no women and lots of long, pointy objects.
* *Pleasure Island.* Enough said.
* *Snow White and the Seven Dwarves.* Sends a positive message about nontraditional families.
* *Swiss Family Treehouse.* Secret hideaway; no telling what goes on there.
* *Tom Sawyer Island.* Boys will be boys.
* *Typhoon Lagoon.* Sight of so many buffed, bronzed bodies wearing Speedos, cavorting in inner tubes, and crashing into each other in wave pools might be too much for straight folks to handle. Everyone out of the pool!
* *Anything* to do with Peter Pan.

This list of suggested attractions and sites to avoid is not inclusive; others may have gay themes or subtexts as well. We apologize for any inconvenience this might cause. We ask those guests' indulgence and invite them to return any other time throughout the year as we—and every resort, theme park, and entertainment destination in the United States—celebrate Straight Day.

Morning Announcements

Attention! Attention, please! Could I have everyone's attention, please, for the morning announcements.

Thank you.

First, a reminder: The Debate Club competes for the league championship at 7:30 this evening, in the small conference room. Everyone is asked to come and support our master debaters.

The Drama Club's production of Tennessee Williams's *Cat on a Hot Tin Roof* will be performed this Friday and Saturday night at 8 o'clock in the auditorium. Please come and support the school thespians.

This next announcement is very important. It concerns every student and teacher, so please listen. I am reading from a note I received yesterday from our district superintendent of schools. It says, and I quote, "According to recent court rulings, harassment of students based on sexual orientation is illegal." So, students, as of today I am officially banning any type of behavior directed against homosexuals or anyone perceived as homosexual.

There is to be no—I repeat, no—tripping or shoving of gay or lesbian students in our hallways. You can't stuff their heads in the toilet, you can't call them names out loud or under your breath, and you can't say you're picking them last in gym class because they're queers. You can't write "So-and-So is a homo" on your desks, or say it on the bus, or anywhere else that has anything to do with school.

Now, this next point I am addressing to the teachers, so stop grading papers or reading the newspaper and pay attention to what I'm saying. No funny comments in class, right? The gay jokes, the limp wrists, the fruitcake stuff—that's all going to end immediately. That's not what this great school is all about. Just remember our school motto: "Respect for learning and love for all." I know you can do it.

Everyone, we've got a fine record at this school of making sure everyone gets along. Let's keep it that way. No ifs, ands, or buts.

Now, one final announcement. Tickets for the annual Snowflake Ball are on sale all week during lunch. The price is $5 each or $7 per couple. So hurry up and find a date!

That's today's morning announcements. Have a great day.

Stonewall Regrets

Thirty years ago, over the course of several hot summer nights, a group of us—drag queens, mostly—battled New York's finest in front of the Stonewall Inn. We threw bottles and rocks; they beat and arrested us. The modern gay rights movement was born.

We're sorry about that.

True, our activism spawned three decades of important social change, but every silver lining has a cloud.

Just think: Had we only kept our mouths shut and gone quietly into those N.Y.P.D. paddy wagons, America would have been spared:

* Ellen
* The terms "post-gay," "gender identity," and "heterosexism"
* *Vanity Fair, Details,* and *GQ*
* Calvin Klein
* The Village People
* Heather's two mommies and Daddy's roommate
* Wigstock
* "Earring magic" Ken
* Circuit parties
* Lilith Fair
* Sex Panic!, ACT UP, and the Lesbian Avengers
* 1-900 numbers
* Agonized discussions over whether we should call ourselves "gay," "gay and lesbian," "gay, lesbian, and bisexual," "gay, lesbian, bisexual, and transgendered," or "queer"
* Internecine warfare between organizations with names like the Human Rights Campaign and the National Gay and Lesbian Task Force, which no one outside of Washington, D.C., can tell apart, anyway
* Anita Bryant
* "Don't ask, don't tell"
* Dykes on Bikes, and the letters to the editor that inevitably follow their appearance in any gay pride parade—both from outraged straight people and gays protesting in outrage that "those bull dykes" do not represent "our community"
* The Sisters of Perpetual Indulgence
* The term "palimony"
* AOL chat rooms
* Michelangelo Signorile

* Antigay ballot initiatives in otherwise-beautiful states like Colorado and Oregon
* Castro clones
* Catfights with civil rights leaders over whether homophobia is worse than, analogous to, or less evil than racism
* Log Cabin Republicans
* Television shows with gay characters who never have sex

Every social movement is affected by the Law of Unintended Consequences. These are some of ours. For inflicting them upon the American public, we apologize. The next time we see a bunch of cops with nightsticks, we promise to shut up and surrender.

Football Without a Helmet
A Speech by Reggie White

I'm sure you know that the average NFL huddle has never been mistaken for a Mensa meeting. Nevertheless, in one 50-minute diatribe I managed to make everyone else in the league—and we're talking guys who have serious difficulty counting to 10, even after you spot them the first nine numbers—look like Nobel physicists. I managed to shove my size-15 cleats so far into my mouth, it took a construction crane to get them out.

I wasn't *trying* to offend people. I mean, when I said that Asians can turn a television into a watch, that white folks are great at building businesses, that Hispanics are gifted at family structures because they can fit 20 or 30 of their people in one house, and that the reason Indians never turned into slaves was because they knew their land and had a talent for sneaking up on people, I was *praising* them. These are strengths, not weaknesses.

I guess my biggest fumble was with the homos. From the reaction I got, you'd think I'd said Troy Aikman was gay. Even the sportswriters vilified me, calling me a bigot, ignorant, and a hypocrite.

In retrospect, calling homosexuality a sin might have been going a little too far. Sins, after all, are serious things. Not keeping the Sabbath, for example, is a sin. You don't see me going out on Sunday afternoon and...

Let me think of another example.

Okay, here's one. Leviticus says, Thou shalt not touch the skin of a dead pig.

Ummm, well, I'm sure I can come up with a good example sooner or later.

But getting back to God. I am an ordained Baptist minister, so I have a direct pipeline to His locker room. It was God's work that healed my bad back. It was God's will that the Green Bay Packers won Super Bowl XXXI. And, apparently, it was God's plan for the Packers to lose in the 1999 playoffs to the 49ers—the *San Francisco* 49ers. God has a well-developed sense of irony.

So I guess from now on, I'll take God at his word when he says to love your fellow man. I just that doesn't mean I have to switch from defensive end to wide receiver.

Wank Me Up

Official statement: Beverly Hills Police Department

Recently Georgios Panayiotou, aka George Michael, was arrested by an undercover officer from the Beverly Hills Police Department for committing a "lewd act" in a rest room at Will Rogers Memorial Park.

Because this area of the park has been the subject of previous lewd-conduct complaints, we undertook surveillance via a four-person unit. The Beverly Hills Police Department is justifiably proud of its large unit.

One of our members was hanging out at the park. That member observed Mr. Michael engaged in a unique one-man arrangement of "Wank Me Up Before You Go-Go," apparently to be followed by a reprise of "I Want My Sex." In other words, Mr. Michael was cleaning his pipes, polishing his Grammy, doin' that crazy hand jive. He was playing the flesh trombone, shaking his maracas, waving his baton—which aroused our undercover member.

Wham! Our agent quickly took matters into his own hands. To his credit, Mr. Michael did not shoot off at the mouth and gave us his John Hancock without a whimper.

We regret that our unit's productivity has been splattered all over the tabloids and talk shows, but we could do little to stop it. When our members come upon well-known individuals, the situation is always sticky.

Because of his high name recognition, arresting him was hard. In the end, we decided this matter was something we could not toss off lightly. But such behavior as exhibited by Mr. Michael is illegal, and we could not allow him to pull it off. He was punished with a stiff fine.

The Beverly Hills Police Department understands that all celebrities need plenty of exposure, plus a little stroking. We do not enjoy arresting them for entertaining themselves. We do, however, ask that they first go through proper channels and obtain all the necessary permits. Even if they are only performing in a tiny one-man show.

Don't Worry, Don't Care

All members of the United States Armed Forces are hereby informed that, effective 0800 hours tomorrow, the United States Department of Defense policy on homosexuality, informally known as "don't ask, don't tell," will be replaced by a new policy. The updated policy will hereafter be referred to as "don't worry, don't care." All versions of the previous policy are to be superseded by the new one.

Under the "don't worry, don't care" policy, no gay, lesbian, bisexual, transgendered, or questioning (henceforth referred to as "homosexual") service member is to worry about his or her sexual orientation. Furthermore, all commanding officers are ordered not to care about the sexual orientation of any personnel under their command.

Homosexual military personnel may now refer to a "lover," "partner," "boyfriend," or "girlfriend" without fear of consequence, just as heterosexual military personnel are permitted to make references to a "husband," "wife," or "bitch."

Homosexual military personnel may now post private E-mail without fear that such correspondence will be used in any manner to embarrass, humiliate, or coerce either the sender or recipient. Suggestive user names such as "Sarge9inchz" and "GenSchlong," however, are inappropriate, as are offers to perform certain actions while on duty. All previous restrictions regarding improper use of military uniforms, facilities, and equipment remain in effect.

Homosexual service members are hereby ordered to cease lying about their sexual orientation. This will bring homosexual personnel into compliance with other regulations regarding honor, integrity, and truthfulness. Military personnel found lying about their sexual orientation may be disciplined for providing false statements. Exceptions may be made for personnel who are genuinely "confused."

The General Accounting Office estimates that the cost of discharging homosexual service members has surpassed $130 million. Thus, implementation of "don't worry, don't care" is expected to free up a substantial sum of money. The Department of Defense has not yet identified projects into which the money will be redirected, but the construction of Stealth Bombers and "stall" showers are expected to top the list.

To reiterate: Under "don't worry, don't care," all homosexual military personnel are hereby ordered to cease any and all feelings of paranoia, isolation, and fear. It is expected that the enormous amount of time, energy, and emotion heretofore invested in hiding sexual orientation; creating fictitious sexual partners and interests; changing pronouns; decorating work and living quarters with "appropriate" photographs, posters, and calendars; and otherwise pretending to be someone one is not while simultaneously guarding against inadvertent disclosures of homosexuality will henceforth be channeled into more efficient pursuits.

"Don't worry, don't care" is being implemented as part of a broad U.S. Department of Defense initiative to welcome the 21st century by becoming part of it. The Department acknowledges that, contrary to previous policy, homosexuality is neither a psychological defect nor a character flaw; that homosexuals are fully capable of performing every task required of military personnel; that homosexuals are not today considered targets of blackmail; and that the presence of openly homosexual service members will not undermine morale. Therefore, effective 0800 hours tomorrow, all military personnel will cease to worry and/or care. And that's an order.

You Got Me, Babe

It's not often that a guy kills himself in a skiing accident (or dies by any means, for that matter) and gets to come back and send a message from beyond. Then again, I'm not just any guy. I'm Sonny Bono. I was, anyway, for 62 years.

I gotta admit, I led a goofy life. I never voted till I was 53, and then I jumped on the ol' entertainer-turned-politician bandwagon and got myself elected mayor of Palm Springs. I'll be the first to say that it wasn't the toughest job around: Singing with Cher was plenty harder. Then I got bored and ran for the senate. U.S. Senate, I think.

The campaign wasn't easy. People asked dumb, intrusive questions, like why was I qualified. So I just told it like it is, er, was. "I don't know what 'qualified' means," I said. "And I think people get too hung up on that in a way, you know?" I lost that race, but two years later I started gigging as a U.S. congressman. I am told that is one notch below senator, but it still seems pretty cool.

Imagine that: Me—a puny first-generation Sicilian-American from Detroit with big teeth and a high, nasal voice—sitting in the Capitol, making speeches and laws, and (my favorite) posing for pictures. I had to trade in my fur vests and bell-bottom pants for some actual suits, but that old stuff was getting a bit raggedy anyway.

Part of my appeal was that I was such a family man. Family, family, family all the way, that was me. In fact, I'm so into family values that my four children came from three of my four wives. Personally, my favorite wife was Mary Whitaker, because when I met her in 1984 she was only 22. That was quite an advantage over Cher, who was getting a bit long in the tooth and who had dumped me besides. Mary was my First Lady in Palm Springs, even if she wasn't exactly my "first lady"! But hey, don't ask, don't tell—that's my philosophy.

Except for one thing: same-sex marriages! That was where I drew the line. In my songbook, marriage is sacred. A man and a woman, not two men and not two women. Till death do us part, or at least until you find another someone younger and prettier!

Some people thought that was wrong. They even brought up Chastity, the daughter I had with, I think, Cher. (Yeah, it was Cher. Now I remember: We got married just after Chastity was born.) I found out Chastity is a lesbian, but even so I loved her to death. (Mine, not hers!) In fact, I loved plenty of lesbians, especially the ones who came to Palm Springs for the Dinah Shore Golf Tournament and spent tons of money. Talk about making a mayor look good!

Still, I co-sponsored legislation to deny federal recognition to same-sex marriages. That didn't go over too good with Chastity or the Dinah Shore crowd, but a man's gotta do what he's gotta do, right?

Now, here in the afterlife—I went straight from skiing at Heavenly Ski Resort to heaven, what a hoot—I'm getting a different view of lesbian love. I've met Gertrude Stein and Eleanor Roosevelt (you coulda knocked me over with a feather!) and my personal fave from the music world, Dusty Springfield. We've had some interesting conversations, and now I'm willing to, as they say, change my tune.

So I'm telling Chastity and all her lesbian friends and all the gay guys I met in my careers in music and the restaurant business (and politics!) that I was wrong. Chastity and everyone else deserves the same opportunity at marriage that I had four times. It's not about gay or straight, it's about what Cher and I sang about incessantly, over and over again: love.

So strike up the band and sing it with me, won't you?

I got you, babe.

The Word of God

Hello down there! This is an old friend speaking! Could I have your attention for a few minutes? This won't take long, but I think it's important.

My name is God, and I'm getting more than a little ticked off at the way my book, the Bible, is being used. You've had crusades, an Inquisition, witch-hunts, and too many schisms to count. You've twisted my words to argue that women are supposed to be subservient to men and white races are supposed to rule the earth. Now you're saying my gay, lesbian, bisexual, and transgendered children are sinners.

Well, read your Bible a little more closely. I don't call homosexuality sinful. Nowhere in my entire book will you find the words gay and sin even close to each other.

Go ahead; check out your sin section. You'll find stealing, cheating, and lying in there. Murder, yes. Adultery too. But not homosexuality. And yet there you folks are, condemning your fellow men and women to hell simply because of who they love.

I know what you're thinking: Sodom. To tell the truth, sometimes I wish I'd never stuck that story in there. If I ever get around to revising the Bible, I'll start by reworking the section on Sodom and Gomorrah, because it's clear I did not edit that part well the first time through. I never meant to convey that the sin of Sodom was homosexuality. Instead, it was pride, excess, and failure to aid the poor and needy. You know, the same sins that pervade much of the world today.

I know what else you're thinking: Leviticus. I'm plum sick and tired of having that book thrown around like a Frisbee at a church picnic. Yes, I talked about a "man lying with another man" as an "abomination," but the idea was for you to go out and procreate and keep the human race alive. Now, several millennia later, you've reproduced like too many Xerox machines. So forget I ever said it.

If I was an evil God, I think I'd hurl a few thunderbolts the next time I heard one of you mention Leviticus. What about the part where I said, "Whatsoever hath no fins or scales in the waters, that shall be an abomination unto you"? I can't remember the last time I heard a televangelist shake his fist at his congregation and tell them to stop eating lobster. And Leviticus mandates death—death!—for cursing your parents. I don't know what I was think-

ing when I dictated that, or when I spoke out against glut-
tony, wearing garments made of different materials, masturbation, and touching the skin of a dead pig.

Obviously the world has changed since my book went to
press. I can't imagine, at the dawn of a new millennium,
chasing down fat people, women in cotton-poly blends,
teenagers who spend too much time in the bathroom, and
football players.

Here's another thing that really frosts my buns. Time
and again you boast I made you in my image. You're right,
of course; all of you are my creations. But if I made you
in my image and I love you, then I also made them in my
image and I love them too. Gay people are not mistakes; I
didn't wander away for a smoke and then come back to suddenly say, "Oh, my God (ha ha!), there are gay people down
there!" I made some folks straight, some folks gay, and I
even made some in-between. It's just like I made people
different colors, sizes, and shapes. I could have made
everyone the same, but then the world would have been a
very boring place.

Before I get back to work, let me give you one final
message: You are all my children.

Now please, grow up!

It's an Apology for *It's Elementary*

Hi, I'm Debra Chasnoff. I spent four years of my life making a documentary film on homophobia in America's primary schools. *It's Elementary: Talking About Gay Issues in School* received plenty of praise from journalists, media executives, and educators alike. Barry Walters of the *San Francisco Examiner* called it "one of the most important films ever devoted to lesbian and gay issues." Mary Bitterman, CEO and president of KQED Inc., a San Francisco public TV and radio broadcaster, described it as "an excellent program done by an accomplished, sensitive filmmaker." The film was lauded by the *Los Angeles Times,* members of the New York and San Francisco school boards, and Bob Chase, president of the National Education Association.

Now, however, thanks to insight provided by groups like the American Family Association and Coral Ridge Ministries, I realize how wrong I was. I had no idea my film would lure youngsters into (in the capitalized words of Coral Ridge Ministries' D. James Kennedy) "ACCEPTANCE of homosexuality." I had no idea that I was introducing children as young as 5 to "deviant sexual behavior." I probably didn't realize this because nowhere in the film is any mention made of sexual activities, not to mention the fact that the intended audience is educators, parents, and other adults, not children. But in retrospect it seems clear that any 5-year-old who happened to catch *It's Elementary* on PBS at 10 or 11 P.M. would be so enthralled by the film's discussion of the prejudice and discrimination gay men and lesbians face that he or she would immediately ACCEPT homosexuality. And from there, it is but a small step to "deviant sexual behavior."

I am sorry the film exposes young children to the concept of homosexuality. Although, judging from comments made by some youngsters in the film about "faggots" and "perverts," some children have heard about homosexuality before. In the long run, though, I agree that it is probably better to shield them from—rather than expose them to—the real world. School is certainly not the place to convey information children might, at some point in their lives, utilize. Heavens! What was I thinking?

I am pleased, however, to report that Donald Wildmon of the American Family Association has developed his own "bibilically [sic] sound" video to counter *It's Elementary.* It's called *Suffer the Children*—talk about an upbeat title! At least he spelled it right.

Kennedy's Coral Ridge Ministries has also made a video. Taking just a few scenes from *It's Elementary,* they manage to make a statement about the entire documentary. For example, after a scene from my film in which a child compares being open-minded to trying a new vegetable, one Coral Ridge parent expostulates, "They're teaching the children to be open-minded. Therefore, you should try things; therefore, you should try to be a homosexual." What brilliant logic! Thanks, guys, for clearing that up.

In conclusion, I apologize for making a film so chock-full of errors, omissions, and evil ideas. I promise to do better with my next film, a documentary on the scheduled Dr. Laura television talk show. I'm calling it *Suffer the Viewers.*

The Adulterous Attorney General
Questions and answers with Michael Bowers, attorney general of Georgia and candidate for governor

Q: Mr. Bowers, during your 16 years as attorney general of the state of Georgia you were a staunch defender of "traditional marriage."

A: That's correct.

Q: And now, in your race for governor, you have admitted that over a 10-year period you violated the vows of your own marriage of more than 30 years by committing adultery. In fact, your adulterous relationship with a woman who worked for you helped destroy her marriage.

A: Unfortunately, that is basically correct too.

Q: As attorney general you carried the *Bowers v. Hardwick* case to the U.S. Supreme Court and successfully defended the case on the basis that sodomy is illegal in the state of Georgia.

A: That is correct.

Q: Adultery is also illegal in this state, sir.

A: I am not aware of any prosecutions for that offense during my tenure.

Q: Were you having an adulterous affair at the time you prosecuted Mr. Hardwick?

A: No comment.

Q: Supporters call your decade-long affair an aberration. Is it?

A: Yes.

Q: Is homosexuality an aberration?

A: No comment.

Q: Sir, Mr. Hardwick was arrested in his own bedroom for having consensual sex with another man after his roommate let a police officer into his home for unrelated reasons. Could you have been arrested for having consensual sex with a woman who was not your wife if a police officer came into your home for unrelated reasons?

A: I will not comment on that.

Q: Mr. Attorney General, in the decision that you won, the Supreme Court ruled that there is no constitutional right to privacy for homosexual activity. Is there a constitutional right to privacy for adulterous heterosexual activity, which is also against the law and is, in fact, the subject of one of the Ten Commandments, while homosexuality is not?

A: I cannot comment specifically on that question.

Q: Did you ever engage in heterosexual sodomy behind closed doors?

A: I will not answer any question like that.

Q: Mr. Bowers, you recently won a federal appeals court victory against Robin Shahar, a lesbian attorney and law clerk, after you withdrew a job offer to her because she was about to have a private commitment ceremony, which you said would have damaged the credibility and effectiveness of your office by flouting the Georgia sodomy law.

A: Is that a question?

Q: No, sir. My question is this: Did *you* damage the credibility and effectiveness of the attorney general's office by flouting the Georgia adultery law?

A: That is a question I will not comment on.

Q: Mr. Attorney General, is "coming out" as an adulterer the same thing as coming out as gay or lesbian?

A: I cannot say. I am not gay.

Q: With regards to the Shahar case, sir, do you think in hindsight you should have fired yourself for committing adultery?

A: No comment.

Q: And regarding the Hardwick case, do you think in hindsight you should have arrested yourself when you realized you were an adulterer?

A: I will not comment on that question.

Q: One last question, sir, if we can...Mr. Bowers, do you consider yourself a hypocrite?

A. I think my actions as attorney general speak for themselves.

Hollywood Star, Actor X

You know me.

For years you've flocked to my movies. I've flown sky-high dogfights, battled enemies foreign and domestic. I've saved countless women from disaster and taken nearly as many to bed. I am cool under fire, suave, and, above all, young and hip. I am macho yet sensitive. I am the envy of males and females alike.

I have become wealthy and famous beyond my wildest dreams. No party is complete until I arrive; no film is a guaranteed blockbuster unless it has my name above the title. I cannot make a move in public without being photographed; I cannot keep my name out of gossip columns.

I also cannot come out as a gay man.

A number of people know my secret: my gay agent; the gay directors I've worked with; the gay heads of studios I've worked for; the gay costume designers, hair stylists, voice coaches, and personal trainers I've met, on sets and off. My boyfriends know too, of course.

And other people wonder. Each week, it seems, an item appears in the *Globe* or *Star,* dropping little hints. And I can't even count the number of Web sites questioning my sexual preference.

Which is why I married my nearly-as-famous, equally closeted girlfriend in a well-publicized wedding. Also why my wife and I have had two well-publicized children. Nothing says "heterosexual" like a beautiful wife and two smiling kids.

This whole charade is silly, I know. Hollywood has long been a haven for gay men. Stars have been jumping in and out of each other's beds for years. And gay characters are now in, right? Straight men are kissing other straight men all over the screen, and no one cares. Every film imaginable has at least one gay guy. So why should I worry about the effect on my career if I came out as a gay man?

Because.

Because the reality of Hollywood today is: When straight men play gay it's called acting, but when gay men play straight it's called "Middle America will never buy it." If you're gay, you can own a studio, write million-dollar screenplays, and compose Academy Award–winning scores. But you can't be a star. At least, that's the prevailing industry wisdom, and no one I know has the courage to test it. Especially me.

I know the incredible effect coming out would have, especially on gay teenagers. I was one myself; I knew half the guys in the theater were just like me, and I knew none of them would ever say it out loud. What I wouldn't have given to have had just one role model! What a difference it would have made in my life!

But there was no one. So I stayed in the very large Drama Club closet. I learned how to act—how to play a role. I learned how to be someone else.

It's funny: My best role—straight boy—is the only part I never wanted to play.

We Have a Dream
A Letter to Alveda King

Dearest Alveda:

None of us is our brother's keeper. Still, as believers in the dream envisioned by your uncle, the Rev. Dr. Martin Luther King Jr., we feel obligated to speak up about your recent homophobic statements.

You have been surprisingly outspoken on the issue of homosexuality. Your position is clear: You oppose it. Further, you oppose all attempts to equate it or any gay rights legislation with the civil rights struggle for which Dr. King gave his life.

Gays and lesbians, you say, do not possess "the innate and immutable" characteristics that mark black people in the fight for equal justice and opportunity. You have said "No one is enslaving the homosexual" and that you have never known "the homosexual community to be lynched, to be bombed...."

You compare homosexuality to obesity, calling both a choice—and claiming you have been denied jobs and mistreated because you are overweight. You argue that neither gays nor heavy people deserve protection against discrimination.

To the gay men and women who say "I was born this way," you reply, "You can be born again." You once told a crowd of 300, "God hates racism, and God hates homosexuality." You say that if your uncle were alive, he would agree with you.

We respectfully disagree.

Dr. King believed, as we do, that injustice anywhere is a threat to justice everywhere, that discrimination against one group is a civil rights issue of concern to all groups.

And for your contention that the gay community has never known lynchings or other types of discrimination, you are horribly wrong. Just ask Matthew Shepard, Billy Jack Gaither, thousands of Holocaust victims, and millions of other nameless, faceless gays, lesbians, bisexuals, and transgendered people. Oh, wait—you can't.

It is clear to us that gay people are not asking for special rights any more than black people—or obese people—are. The demand is for equal rights. Bigotry is always bigotry; discrimination remains discrimination. Dr. King embraced and articulated that heartfelt core concept clearly and constantly.

Therefore, on Dr. King's behalf, we—the friends, family, and followers of the teachings of Dr. Martin Luther King—respectfully request of you, Alveda King, the following: Hush up!

Yours truly,
The Dreamers of the World

Confessions of an Ex–Ex-Gay

Not too many years ago, doctors, ministers, and other supposedly learned folk labored mightily to cure human beings of a pleasurable, yet potentially deadly, sin. They failed, of course, because the "lethal" behavior was basic human drive. Today, happily, Americans of all ages are free to indulge, relatively guilt-free, in the delights of masturbation.

Unhappily, a new generation of moralists has discovered another potentially deadly sin against which to preach: homosexuality. The sons of the men who preached sermons, devised mechanical devices, even invented Corn Flakes to cure masturbation, have taken aim at the sons (and daughters) of masturbators. Their weapons are the same—scare tactics camouflaged by words of compassion and love—but the stakes are far higher. Where the miscreants of the past feared disease, hairy palms, and flagging erections, today's "sinners" risk losing the two most important characteristics any human being can possess: self-esteem and faith.

I know. I was a gay man. Then I became an ex-gay. Then, thankfully, I became an ex–ex-gay. Along the road to becoming an ex–ex-gay, I have learned many things. Contrary to the lessons preached to me in reparative (conversion) therapy, I now know:

* *Homosexuality cannot be changed.* It is an immutable, innate—and, when you come right down to it, indescribably wonderful—part of who I am. I can change my sexual behavior, just as I can change my right-handedness (by awkwardly using my left) or my blue eyes (slipping on hazel contact lenses). But as soon as I am alone, I will revert to being a righty; as soon as I take out my lenses, I am back to being blue-eyed. Outside appearances mean nothing; it is what's inside our hearts and souls that truly counts.

* *Misinformation and pseudoscience are dangerous.* I was lucky; I became an ex-gay as an adult. Despite being sucked into the ex-gay movement, I was intelligent enough and mature enough to eventually recognize false words and unverifiable facts for what they were. Young people are less able to do this. They are more vulnerable to phony promises, snake oil, and contradictions of medical, psychological, psychiatric, epidemiological, sociological, and statistical experts. I feel for them, and I firmly believe that what the ex-gay movement is doing to young people qualifies as child abuse.

* *People do struggle with homosexuality—but the struggle arises from society's reactions to homosexuals, not from within.* If certain segments of society—the religious right in particular—did not demonize homosexuality, there would be no reason for gays to "struggle" with who they are. Ex-gay organizations prey on homosexuals' inner torment—torment that is caused by the very people who hold it up as an example of the reason we "must" change.

* *When the ex-gay ministries say "If you really love someone, you'll tell them the truth," it is clear that they do not know much about either.* Love means accepting another person for who he or she is; truth means not using other people for dubious ends—in the ex-gay ministries, this means raising money for political power. The ex-gay movement is closely aligned with the religious right. *That* is the truth, and it has nothing whatsoever to do with love.

* *Prayer works only when one prays for the right reason.* A person cannot pray to be cured of something that is not a disease in the first place. Because God made all people in his image, it is clear that he made me gay. Therefore, instead of praying for change, I should pray for the gift of understanding, accepting, and loving myself.

* *The number of ex–ex-gays is nearly as great as the number of ex-gays.* Studies show that few people remain ex-gays for long. Even the founders of one ex-gay organization—Exodus International—have renounced the concept. When they realized the ministry was harming many more people than it helped, and they saw the statistics on ex-gays who were attempting suicide or becoming clinically depressed, they began to speak out against such ministries. (It hardly helped that they had also fallen in love!)

* *Sigmund Freud was no fool.* The father of psychoanalysis said, "In general, to undertake to convert a fully developed homosexual into a heterosexual is not much more promising than to do the reverse." One wonders at the reaction if an organization spent millions of dollars on television and print ads to try to convert the leaders of the ex-gay ministries into homosexuals! (On a less flippant note, one should ask the ex-gay leaders two obvious questions: When did they choose their heterosexuality? And, if they wanted to, could they change?)

* *Ex-gay ministers seem to have an unhealthy preoccupation with homosexuality.* When you come right down to it, you have to think: Why do these people care so much about our sex lives? What motivates them to preach so long and loud about what we do in the privacy of our bedrooms? Don't they seem just a little *too* interested?

* *Homosexuality is not just about sex. It is about joy and love and acceptance.* Spending any amount of time in an ex-gay ministry, in a futile attempt to change one's sexual fantasies and behavior, is an enormous waste of energy and emotion. Far better to spend the limited amount of time each of us has on this earth seeking out those other human beings who can provide us with happiness, who can make us feel whole and complete and loved—who can give us *hope*—than in a hopeless endeavor.

Having learned these lessons—the hard way—I apologize. I apologize for turning my back on my friends in the gay community. I apologize to my parents and family for letting them believe I could "change." I apologize to myself for ever believing that I was an unworthy human being.

But apologies belong in the past. Today I look ahead and see a bright future. And, I am happy to say, I do so as an open, proud—and ex-*straight*—man.

A Special Plea From Anita

It might seem strange for someone with my background—Miss Oklahoma of 1958, Miss America second runner-up of 1959, entertainer and spokesperson for Florida orange juice—to have battled the homosexual community. In 1977, however, it seemed like a sweet career move. I was no great shakes as a singer, and people were willing to spend only so many hours a day discussing o.j. (These were the halcyon days before Americans spent an entire year talking about O.J.)

So when the Dade County Commission became one of the first legislative bodies in the country to pass an ordinance making it illegal to discriminate on the basis of sexual orientation, I peeled into action. Giving civil rights to homosexuals, I knew, was the first step on the road toward the end of America as a Christian nation. That fact was as plain as the nose on my still-pretty face. So I organized a group called Save Our Children. A referendum was held, and the intelligent citizens of Dade County voted to overturn the ordinance.

Save Our Children was a success. I was more famous than ever. I took my show on the road, helping citizens successfully oppose gay rights laws wherever they reared their ugly, dangerous heads. From St. Paul, Minn., to Wichita, Kan., to Eugene, Ore., I brought my common-sense appeal.

Unfortunately, Save Our Children served as a wake-up call to homosexual activists all across the country. I was denounced as a bigot. I was hit in the face with a pie at a press conference. And I was canned from my job as a spokesperson for Florida orange juice.

Save Our Children made me a star briefly, and then I tumbled back to earth, out of the public eye. I've fallen so far that in 1998 my theater in Branson, Mo., closed and my husband and I filed for bankruptcy. Even country music fans have turned their backs on me. But rather than sit in my kitchen drinking orange juice and contemplating my navel, I've formed a new organization: Save My Career. Please join or send a contribution today.

Dumb and DOMA
A Letter from Congressman Bob Barr

Dear Constituents:

As a congressman who has always declared how important it is to have the courage of one's convictions, it is not easy to admit a mistake. But I made a big one recently, and it has affected many people. I guess if you hang around with rock-ribbed conservatives for too long, you get rocks in your head. How else to explain how hard-headed and wrong I have been on this whole gay marriage issue?

I authored and supported DOMA, as it is popularly called. The law defines marriage, for federal purposes, as meaning "only a legal union between one man and one woman as husband and wife." The act also excuses each state from having to follow the "full faith and credit" clause of the U.S. Constitution. In other words, any state may refuse to recognize a marriage made in another state if that other state does not comply with its definition of marriage. The bill passed overwhelmingly in 1996 and was signed by President Clinton. So far 34 states have introduced their own DOMA laws, just in case our federal bill does not pass constitutional muster.

Not until a trusted longtime aide on the Hill came out as gay did I grasp a fundamental point: DOMA completely contradicts the most basic of all conservative principles—government should keep its nose out of private citizens' lives. I have spent my entire career arguing for less government intervention and more personal freedom, and there I was standing up on the floor of Congress advocating for more government control and less liberty. If that is not a hypocritical position, I don't know what is.

I was wrong on DOMA on a number of counts. I apologize first and foremost to one of my political heroes, Sen. Phil Gramm of Texas, who was just as avid a DOMA supporter as I. A strict reading of DOMA shows that giving individual states the power to regulate marriages made in other states would allow laws against interracial marriage to stand. That would prove problematic indeed for Senator Gramm and his second wife, a Korean woman.

My opposition to gay marriage and authorship of DOMA would have the effect of denying basic rights to one group of people—a group that includes my gay aide. After having argued for the rights of hunters and cigarette smokers, it seems ridiculous for me to argue against the rights of gay men and women. They too deserve the chance at enjoying socially sanctioned and fully recognized lives together.

By not being allowed to marry, gay people do not enjoy the advantages other Americans do—and to those of us who believe in the American dream, that is distinctly un-American. DOMA effectively prohibits gay men and women from filing joint tax returns, claiming federal employee and health benefits, and receiving Social Security survivors' benefits. Now, I am as opposed to governmental handouts as any conservative, but if we've got a program in place, it ought to be open to all. And that includes my homosexual staff member.

I have heard a number of arguments against gay marriage. I now see how fallacious they are.

It is said, for example, that allowing gay people to wed would destroy the sacred institution of marriage. The list of fellow DOMA supporters who have not treated their wedding vows as sacred is headed by Newt Gingrich, who went to the hospital where his first wife was undergoing cancer treatment to inform her that he was leaving. Several years later he dumped wife number 2 over the telephone. The reason for his second divorce was his involvement in a four-year affair with a congressional aide, a woman 23 years his junior.

Newt's serial divorces are perhaps the most egregious examples of marital hypocrisy, but he is not alone. I, for instance, have been married three times and was caught licking whipped cream off the chests of two women who were not my wives.

Another common argument is that gays should not marry because they do not procreate. Neither have Bob and Libby Dole, nor Pat and Shelley Buchanan. Not to mention the fact that many gay people do have children.

It is further said that allowing gays to marry gives them special rights. As a staunch conservative, I firmly oppose any such treatment. However, "special" rights means exempting someone from something or granting something extra other citizens do not have. That does not seem to be the case here.

Some of my more religious friends have noted that the Bible forbids gay marriage. In fact, the good book says nothing about marriage. There's not enough room in it for that, filled as it is with injunctions against hypocrisy and judging others, and advice about love, tolerance, and fighting injustice wherever it occurs.

However, even I must admit that the DOMA legislation was not entirely without merit. It passed with such overwhelming majorities in both houses of Congress that President Clinton (who has never taken his own marital vows too literally) was pressured into signing it. In order to minimize news coverage he put his signature on the bill in the dead of night. The ploy did not work; in fact, he was sharply criticized by his supporters for signing it at all and by his opponents for trying to hide what he did.

Anything that makes him look bad, I like. After all, I'm still a conservative. In fact, by changing my stance on DOMA I'm acting more conservatively than ever.

Sincerely Yours,
Bob Barr

Funny Girl, Ellen DeGeneres

I'm a funny lady. I once won an American Comedy Award as Funniest Female Performer in a TV special. I was named Showtime's Funniest Person in America back in 1982. I finished 29th on *Entertainment Weekly*'s list of the "50 Funniest People Alive," although, personally, I do not believe Homer Simpson, Beavis, or Butthead are technically "alive." Furthermore, I am the only female comic to be invited to sit on Johnny Carson's couch during her first appearance.

So yes, I am a funny female. Funny in the traditional sense, and also, if you haven't heard, "funny that way."

When my character, Ellen Morgan, came out on my TV show, *Ellen,* in 1997 (and I did the same thing in real life), about 40 million people watched. I was on the cover of *Time* magazine and would have made the front of *Newsweek* too if not for that silly Heaven's Gate mass suicide; there were coming-out parties in thousands of living rooms and dyke bars across America. Comedian Elvira Kurt said, "It's like Courtney Love playing a heroin addict. Ellen playing a lesbian. What range! How does she do it?"

Not unexpectedly, a few sponsors had problems. Chrysler, General Motors, J.C. Penney, and Johnson & Johnson all bailed out—based, I suppose, on the flawless logic that only gay people would watch the show and that gay people don't buy cars, trucks, bras, or shampoo. Olivia cruises jumped into the breach, but ABC decided their ads were too—what, cruisy?—to broadcast.

The Baptist Church announced a boycott—as if they watched *Ellen* before—but America's top TV critic, Dan Quayle, was strangely silent. A few years earlier the then–vice president had confused Murphy Brown with a real person, but this time he had nothing to say.

Then again, Quayle and the Republicans were no longer in power. That's why I got invited to the White House, along with my former main squeeze Anne Heche. I am happy to report that although there were plenty of women around, I was not tempted at all. None of the interns was my type.

And then a year later I got canned. That's not a lesbian term for some weird type of sex; it's a synonym for "screwed; not renewed." I was replaced in mid–sweeps month by *Two Guys, A Girl, And a Pizza Place.* It took five people and a hunk of mozzarella to replace me. Better to air a show about anchovies than watch me kiss another woman during a commitment ceremony.

I took plenty of heat from people who said *Ellen* had suddenly become unfunny, who said *Ellen* was "too gay."

Hello? *Ellen* was too gay? Has anyone actually been watching television for the past 30 years? I mean, has no show ever centered on a lead character's *hetero*sexuality?

I refuse to apologize for being "too gay." But in lieu of an apology, I will share with you the plot summaries of all the episodes we'd planned that never made it to air.

* Ellen sells her bookstore and becomes a professional golfer
* Ellen runs off with Roseanne
* Ellen and Flip Wilson give each other fashion tips
* Ellen announces, "I Love Lucy."
* Ellen moves to Minneapolis to live with Mary Tyler Moore
* Ellen hangs out with The Golden Girls
* Ellen gets a job at Cheers and helps Diane discover her true sexuality
* Ellen runs off with Xena: Warrior Princess
* Ellen starts a new career as a lifeguard on *Baywatch*
* *Bosom Buddies.* Enough said
* Ellen tries to "change" by boarding *The Love Boat*
* Ellen gets set up on a blind date with Frasier
* Ellen hosts *This Old House*
* Ellen makes a guest appearance on *The Facts of Life*
* Ellen goes to a MASH unit and helps Hot Lips Houlihan discover her true sexuality
* Ellen experiments with new careers, as the Bionic Woman, the Flying Nun, and Alice
* Ellen changes the name of her show to the more apt *Leave It to Beaver*

All of those shows, of course, would have the advantage of one sponsor eager to hop aboard the post-Ellen bandwagon: Snap-On tools.

Those Boys in the Band

Today, most Americans don't know the name Mart Crowley. Even among gay people, I'm more the answer to a trivia question than a noted icon. But 30 years ago I wrote one of the most controversial plays of all time, *The Boys in the Band*. One thing is certain: *The Boys in the Band* would never pass muster with today's PC police.

Set in the late 1960s, the play (and subsequent movie) involves a circle of aging gay friends who gather in Greenwich Village for a birthday party. All the major subgroups except leather are represented: the butch teacher, the fashion photographer, the poodle-walking decorator, the slow-witted hustler, the unhappy couple. The evening is filled with dancing, drinking, and bitterness, capped by one man's nervous breakdown. The "boys in the band" were a spectacular assemblage of neurotically entangled flaming queens and quivering closet cases.

The self-esteem of that fictitious gang of gays was lower than the Reverend Phelps's rating on the Kinsey Scale. Impressionable gay men who saw either the stage or screen version moved deeper into the shadows, or hustled off to therapy, in an era when homosexuality was still classified as a mental illness. They hated themselves, their sexuality, and the society that hated them. Uplifted they were not.

"Show me a happy homosexual and I'll show you a gay corpse," said Michael, the party's host, in a line still parroted by homophobes as "proof" that gay people really want to change. Another character says, "If we could just learn not to hate ourselves quite so very much."

Critics complained *The Boys in the Band,* particularly its culture of youth, materialism, substance abuse, and promiscuity, pushed the gay movement back 20 years. Others said it actually advanced the gay cause: Gay men grew so revolted by the picture I painted, they resolved to change the gay world. I'm not sure how accurate that is, but the Stonewall riots occurred just a year after my play debuted off-Broadway. Coincidence?

And anyway, what do you expect from gay theater back in 1968—especially from a playwright born in Vicksburg, Miss., and educated at the Catholic University in Washington, D.C.? You write what you know, and that's what I did.

At least *The Boys in the Band* was marketed as fiction. That's a lot more than you can say for *Everything You Always Wanted to Know About Sex** (**But Were Afraid to Ask)*, written by Dr. David Reuben at roughly the same time. According to him, homosexuality was immoral, perverted, and grotesque. Compare the number of gay teenagers who furtively flipped through that best-seller seeking information on homosexuality with the number of gay men who saw *The Boys in the Band,* and I suspect you'll find that Dr. Reuben lowered more homosexuals' self-esteem than I ever did.

Besides, I'm only a playwright. He's a doctor! And 30 years later he's still dispensing advice. At least I've had the good sense to lay low.

Southern Fried Baptists

Dear God:

I'm writing to ask about this Southern Baptists boycott of the Walt Disney Company for its "gay friendly" activities and policies. I just don't understand. The whole thing seems so Mickey Mouse.

Disney is gay? How Goofy can that be?

It all started when "The Lion King" came out. People worried that Timon and Pumba were lovers. I didn't even know meerkats and warthogs could be gay! That got me thinking about other Disney stars and wondering if they were gay. If they are, they pretty much keep their sex lives private. What they do in the privacy of their jungles or forests or ponds or hutches is their own business.

Still, our leaders have asked us to boycott all of Disney. It would have been a lot easier for them to request that we try to eliminate poverty or disease! Besides Disney World and Disneyland and all those Disney and Miramax movies and Discover magazine and the A&E network and ABC, Disney also owns ESPN. Giving up Ted Koppel and "Who Wants to Be a Millionaire" is one thing; passing up NASCAR racing and Sports Center is a whole different ball game.

I think the thing that really ticked off some of the Southern Baptists' leaders the most was when Disney extended economic benefits to the partners of its gay employees. That was the straw that broke the camel's back. It seems to me, though, that two gay people who love each other ought to be able to get the same dental deals as two straight people who love each other, especially from a "family-friendly" company like Disney. I've been looking all through the Bible, and I couldn't find anyplace where you talked about hating people who loved each other. I did see where you said "Judge not, lest ye be judged." Great line!

Sometimes, God, I think we Southern Baptists are only living in one section of Disney World: Fantasyland. At this rate we'll never reach Tomorrowland.

God, my Southern Baptist brothers and sisters tell me if I don't boycott the Disney Company and stop the moral decline of America, I'm going to hell. Well, the hell with them. I'm going to Disney World!

Signed,
A Southern Baptist friend

Our Place at the Table
An Apology from the Human Rights Campaign

All right, we'll admit it: We didn't care that much about the endorsement. What we really wanted was "a place at the table."

"The endorsement," of course, is our October 1998 support of Alfonse D'Amato in the New York U.S. Senate race. Our board of directors voted 15–7 to endorse incumbent Senator D'Amato over challenger and longtime gay rights supporter Charles Schumer, a move that ticked off just about everyone: the Clinton White House, Mr. Schumer, and even our own members. Some, including one board director, resigned in protest.

In our defense, we'd like to remind you that politics leads to very strange bedfellows. This time HRC crawled in bed with a man who is not particularly attractive—on any level—in hopes that our liaison would lead to favors down the road. In the end, we got what we deserved. We'd rather not say what that is, but it starts with *f* and ends with *ed*.

We had, we must admit, great self-interest in Senator D'Amato's reelection. We figured that if he won, the HRC would have a marker to cash in later with the Republican Party. Consequently we would gain influence, even power, in Republican circles. Never mind that Senator D'Amato's reelection would have pushed the Republicans closer to a veto-proof majority, in which case our influence would have been meaningless.

We also thought an HRC endorsement would be a way of showing our nonpartisan stance, somehow forgetting that by our very nature we are a partisan organization. For gay and lesbian civil rights. Against bigotry.

And a fat lot of good our endorsement did anyway. Only 14% of gay voters pulled Mr. D'Amato's lever. He didn't do very well with heteros either: Mr. Schumer won the seat by a solid 10% margin. So not only did we upset a good and loyal friend, we threw our weight behind a loser, showing our irrelevance in terms of swaying the outcome of an election. Not bad for one stupid endorsement.

We tried hard to trumpet Senator D'Amato's stands on gay rights. After all, he cosponsored the Employment Non-Discrimination Act, he supported gays in the military, and he spoke in favor of the nomination of James Hormel as ambassador to Luxembourg. Our executive director, Elizabeth Birch, went so far as to tell New Yorkers that they "didn't know" Senator D'Amato's record.

Apparently voters knew all too well. They knew Senator D'Amato had a 75% favorable voting record on gay and lesbian issues and that Representative Schumer had a 100% favorable record. They also knew the Christian Coalition had given Senator D'Amato an 82% favorable rating.

In conclusion, we'd like to say that we never really liked Senator D'Amato, nor did we appreciate his lukewarm embrace of our community. We simply were delighted to find a Republican who did not hate us and who might have served our interests sometime down the line. We really wanted to dine at his table. In the future, though, rather than wheedle seats where we're not wanted, we'll do what we should have done all along. We'll help build a new table—with seats for everyone.

Tinky Talks!

Hi, kids!

Normally I communicate with you in chirps and beeps, and you sort of gurgle back at me, but the time has come in your young lives to know something about me, so I'm sending you this message in plain English. It's important, so please stop bouncing up and down and drooling, and listen.

I'm not gay.

That's right. Despite what the Rev. Jerry Falwell thinks—you know, that strange man with the nice smile who says all those mean things—I am not a homosexual. It doesn't matter if you don't know what "gay" or "homosexual" means. It just matters—apparently—that you know I'm not.

The reverend Falwell *thought* I was gay for a few dumb reasons. Reason number 1: I am purple. The silly Reverend Falwell thought *purple* was "the gay pride color." It's actually *pink,* and maybe lavender too. Do you know the difference between pink and lavender and purple? Probably not; you don't even know the difference between red and blue. But the Reverend Falwell should know the difference, right? He's a grown-up! So it's kind of funny he made that mistake, don't you think? I sure do!

Then the Reverend Falwell said he thought I was gay because my antenna is shaped like a triangle, which is the gay pride symbol. Jeepers creepers! One of the other Teletubbies' antennas looks like an exotic sex toy, but did the Reverend Falwell say anything about *that*? No-o-o.

Anyway, did you kids know the triangle is a gay pride symbol? Of course not. You don't even know what a triangle is, let alone gay pride. And you know what? A lot of *adults* don't even know that the triangle is a gay symbol. (It came from the Nazis, in case you're interested. You'll learn about the Nazis in school about 10 years from now. They're bad people—like the Reverend Falwell but more overt. You'll learn what *overt* means in school too.)

The Reverend Falwell also thought I was gay because I carry a purse. First of all, it's not a purse, it's a magic bag. (Even you knew that!) And why does he assume I'm a boy? My voice is pretty high for a boy. Maybe the Reverend Falwell thinks I haven't hit puberty yet. (Your mommy or daddy or caregiver will tell you about that some day too. If you want a good laugh, ask them about it as soon as you can talk!)

But do you even think Teletubbies can be boys or girls? (Do you want to learn a big word? We call the differences between boys and girls "gender"!) I don't think Teletubbies have gender. I'm a Teletubby, and I don't know if I'm a boy or girl. Maybe that's another reason the Reverend Falwell thinks I'm gay? Oh, well.

Hopefully, when you're a little older and understand the concept of sexuality, you can clue the Reverend Falwell in to the fact that Teletubbies don't have any, one way or the other. That's because—and this is a tough thing to explain to him, but you understand because you're infants—we are *cartoon characters*! Just like Rugrats and Smurfs and Jar Jar Binks. You want to have fun? Let's tell that to the Reverend Falwell and see him have a coronary.

So even though you don't know what "gay" means, let me say it once again, because as your Teletubby friend, I know you have the attention span of a goldfish: I am not gay. If I was gay, I wouldn't look like I've never seen the inside of a gym. I wouldn't wear these silly shoes. (They're not even pumps!) And I definitely would not dress all in *purple*.

Thanks for listening, kids. That *was* important, wasn't it? Now you can go back to doing what you do best. Fall down on the carpet, onto your face. Spit up. And poop!

Burning Down the Log Cabin

And to think we thought you could be both gay and Republican.

As members of the Log Cabin Republicans, we have spent years crawling into bed with the most odious of people: men and women who, when not making speeches denouncing us on the floors of national and state legislatures or at VFW halls and fund-raising dinners across the nation, are doing their darnedest to craft and pass bills that would take away what few rights we now enjoy or make damn sure we don't get any more than we already have.

As Log Cabin Republicans, we share a party with Trent Lott. He is the man who compared homosexuality to klepto-mania and alcoholism. He also said, in opposing antidis-crimination laws for gay and lesbian workers, that such legislation was "part of a larger and more audacious effort to make the public accept behavior that most Americans consider dangerous, unhealthy, or just plain wrong." We would have liked to have had an opportunity to change our fellow Republican's mind, but, to our chagrin, we were unable to argue our position effectively. Though he is the Senate majority leader, he has never once met with us.

Of course, he is not the only Republican leader to avoid the Log Cabin Republicans as if we had the plague—most, no doubt, are sure we do. We have gotten used to watching members of our party freeze when we walk in the room. We know they avoid our calls and send junior aides to meet with our most senior members. A lot of those same legis-lators employ gay men and women on their staffs. A few of them are even gay themselves. Yet they still have no clue who we are, what issues we're fighting for, or why our rights should matter so much to a party that prides itself on defending individual freedom.

Many of our fellow Republicans say that while they like us as individual human beings, they sure would not want us to be their sons' teachers. A congressman once asked our Log Cabin president, "You would never want to be a Boy Scout leader, right?" (We wonder if he knew that the Boy Scouts have already made certain he won't be.)

Some legislators meet with us privately, assure us of their backing, then tell us there will be no public men-tion of that support or even of our meeting. We accepted such closed-door, hush-hush meetings as the price we had to pay for access to power, even within our own party. For instance, we once gave a donation to presidential hopeful Bob Dole. He was delighted to receive it—until word leaked to the press. Then he was shocked—shocked!—and stated quite loudly that our Republican money was not quite appropriate for him. Perhaps it was the first time in our nation's history that a political candidate turned down money. We whimpered a bit, then skulked away with our tail between our legs. Abraham Lincoln would not have been proud.

For that matter, The Great Emancipator and log cabin-born founder of our party might not have been terribly proud of our organization's decision to honor civil rights foe Ward Connerly at our national convention. We gave him our Spirit of Lincoln Award for his support of same-sex domestic-partnership benefits—despite his leadership in favor of California's Proposition 209, which aimed to dismantle all affirmative action programs in public employment, contracting, and education in the state.

The Republican Party likes to style itself as "the big tent," claiming that all are welcome inside. Talk is cheap, however. Steve Forbes flatly opposes any concessions to gay voters. Orrin Hatch, in his recent presidential campaign, told Republicans in his home state of Utah that they could be proud because "we don't have the gays and lesbians with us." Senator Hatch explained his ugly remark by saying, "Gays and lesbians, by and large, are very intelligent, highly educated, high-earning people ." Why on earth, we wonder, would "very intelligent, highly educated, high-earning people" be a group the Republicans would not lust after? So much for the big tent!

At the Republican state convention in Texas, although the party was represented by over 50 elected openly gay delegates and alternates, party leaders denied the Log Cabin Republicans exhibit space. An official statement compared us to the Ku Klux Klan and pedophiles. Like Senator Dole's repudiation of our donation, the Texas Republicans' refusal to rent us space at their convention shows that they put principle over money. That would ordinarily be praiseworthy, except their principle is "We don't want your kind."

Despite inclusive rhetoric, our Republican Party has not included our issues in most of their votes. From 1995, when our party took control of the House, to 1998, Democrats supported gay issues 71% of the time, Republicans only 10%. The ratio in the Senate is nearly as bad: Democrats voted for pro-gay legislation 75% of the time, Republicans only 29%.

Certainly, we Log Cabin Republicans have not exactly helped our cause. For example, in California we endorsed Republican U.S. Senate candidate Matt Fong over pro-gay incumbent Barbara Boxer. That's natural—we're Republicans, after all—but then Mr. Fong donated $50,000 to the

Traditional Values Coalition, an organization dedicated to eradicating gay people from American life.

Well, we are no longer willing to be cowed, crushed, or swept off the planet. We do not even wish to be Republicans any more. We're tired of living in our log cabin closet. It's time we came out and recognized the truth: It's impossible to be both a Republican and a gay person. From now on, we're Democrats. We're trading in the Republican elephant for a Democratic donkey. Call us asses, if you will, for sticking with the Log Cabin Republicans for so long—just let us into your tent. Please.

Happy days are here again!

I Was Such an Idiot

Dear Mark:

You're probably pretty surprised to get this letter from me after so many years. Well, I'm pretty surprised to be writing it. A lot has happened since we grew up on the same street and went through school together. In looking back on my life, I feel ashamed for a lot of the things I did then.

I remember in first grade you wanted to sit next to me on the bus. I said, "E-e-ew, no, get away from me!" and made a big show of changing my seat. I tried to do the same thing in class, but Mrs. Lee wouldn't let me. So I stole your favorite teddy bear, the one you brought in for show-and-tell. I'm sure you guessed it was me, but you never tattled. Maybe you were scared of me, but you were probably just trying to act nice, the way you always did.

In second grade I made fun of you in camp because you always wanted to do "nature" when the rest of us wanted to play baseball or go swimming. One day, to show they were being fair, the counselors said we had to do nature. I was the one who killed all those butterflies you were so proud of. You thought it was Jeff. I remember someone told you I did it, but you said you didn't believe them because I was your friend.

Remember in third grade when I drew that picture of you and your dog right after it got hit by the car? I wrote underneath MARK HAD SEX WITH SCOOTER and passed it around the classroom. I didn't even know what "having sex" meant. Glenn dared me to do it, so I did.

In fourth grade I always made fun of you for playing with the girls during recess. At the time the guys thought that was pretty weird. Now I realize the girls were the only kids in school who talked to you.

Then in fifth grade I threw the ball at your head in Bombardment and laughed when you cried. The next year, in sixth, I was gym captain and got to pick teams. You weren't the most unathletic kid—although you threw like a girl, you were pretty fast—but you kept telling people we were friends because we lived two houses down from each other, and I didn't want them to think we were. So I purposely never picked you. One day you had to be on my team because no one was left. I said, "Coach, do I have to have that mommy's boy?" Today, I can't believe what Coach said: "Well, he has to be on somebody's team, right?" Back then, it seemed like a normal thing for him to say.

The first week of seventh grade, all the guys on the street had a camp-out in Rick's backyard. We started fooling around with each other, and I remember thinking it was kind of fun—no one had ever touched me down there before, and it felt good! But at the same time those feelings confused me, so the next day I told everyone that you tried to kiss me when you thought I was asleep. You did-n't, of course, but no one ever listened to you. I knew they'd believe whatever I said, especially if it was a story about "Mark the mommy's boy."

I have no idea why I did what I did in eighth grade: Out of the blue in the locker room I yelled "Quit looking at me, Mark!" Probably all of us were looking all the time, trying to see if we were as normal as everyone else, but some-how it just popped into my head to say that about you. I think you got some kind of medical excuse not to do gym anymore, and it ended up you had to take a special summer school class instead of going to that art camp you had talked about all year. I bet that really hurt, but you never said anything to anyone about it.

In ninth grade during the trip to Washington, you wrote me down as the person you wanted to room with. I was pissed when I found out and even madder when they wouldn't let me change. I made you sleep on the floor and threatened to rub Ben-Gay on your balls if you got up during the night. You kept wanting to talk after we turned the lights out, but I pretended I was asleep.

The next year we didn't see each other much, but I still managed to torment you. I was the one who wrote *PRODUCED BY MARK THE FAGGOT* all over your art project just before you were supposed to turn it in. I never heard what happened afterward. I kept expecting everyone in school to talk about it, but no one did. By that time you had a few close friends, which surprised me. I'd never seen you with anyone before, except when you hung around us trying to fit in. And then, all of a sudden, there you were in the halls, laughing and joking around. I remember thinking to myself, "Don't those kids know he's a fag?"

In 11th grade you suddenly got really popular, and one day after football practice somebody suggested we teach you a lesson. It wasn't my idea to shove you into the boys' room urinal, but I was there when it happened. And I was one of the five guys who had just taken a leak in it. I'll never forget the look in your eyes when you saw me standing in the back of the crowd. You didn't know the other guys, but you'd known me ever since we played in your sandbox together.

And then in 12th grade I remember the day you came back to school after being in the hospital for trying to kill yourself. No one was supposed to say anything, but I stood in back of you in the cafeteria line and said, "I'd try to kill myself too if I was a homo." It was loud enough for you to hear, but there was a lot of talking going on in line. I thought to myself: "This is so weird. Part of me hopes he heard what I said, but part of me doesn't." I couldn't figure out what I was thinking then.

Through all that stuff, from first grade through senior year, you always wanted to be my friend. Even when I was harassing you the most, you tried to hang out with me—until the urinal incident, anyway. Looking back, I can't believe how meanly I acted——or how normal what I did seemed at the time.

Sometimes, if no one else was around, I said "Hi" in the halls. Your face lit up like a Christmas tree. I knew I had power over you, and it made me feel important. For all the years I used that power the wrong way, I apologize. I'm sorry for all the pain I put you through. I just wasn't able to handle anyone who acted differently, and I was too worried about being cool to think about your feelings. All I thought about was myself.

After your parents moved away they kept in touch with my parents. So I know you live in San Francisco now and you own an art gallery. I'm glad you're doing what you love. I've gotten interested in art, believe it or not, and maybe if I ever get out there you can give me a tour.

My parents also told me you had a partner for more than 10 years but he died. I'm sorry to hear that. I'm glad you had at least a few good years with someone you loved.

Mark, you're probably wondering why I'm writing this long letter now out of the blue after so many years. Well, I have something to confess. My daughter Margo is a lesbian.

I'll spare you the details, but I will tell you this: When I told Mom, her reaction was a lot better than mine. "I guessed that a long time ago," she said. "So what's the big deal?" And then she said, "Remember Mark? He's gay, and he's wonderful. In fact, when you two boys were growing up, sometimes I thought he was a lot nicer than you were."

This might surprise you, Mark, but since high school I've become quite a reader. So I went out and bought books. I discovered a lot of things about homosexuality I never knew. I learned a lot about Margo and also about you. In the process I learned a lot about myself too. I could blame the way I treated you on society or my teachers and coaches and teammates, but that would be a cop-out. In the end, we are all responsible for our own actions and lives.

So that's why I'm writing. I was an idiot when we were growing up. I want to apologize for the stupid things I've done. I want to let you know I hope you are doing well now. And I want to ask, after all those years you spent wanting to be my friend: Can I be yours?

Love,
Doug

I Apologize
An Apology from the Rev. Fred Phelps

I apologize.

I apologize for flying the American flag upside down, below the flag of Zimbabwe, and for stating that Zimbabwean president Robert Mugabe is the only leader of a modern state "taking the proper position on the homosexual menace." I apologize for sullying Memorial Day by claiming that America's veterans "died in vain for a filthy Sodomite nation led by perverts and whores."

I apologize for disrupting gay pride parades across the country. I diminished these days of celebration, sparked prejudice and bigotry in impressionable straight people, and evoked confusion, shame, and self-loathing in young gays and lesbians.

I apologize for picketing the funerals of gay men who have died of AIDS as well as Sen. Barry Goldwater's because he supported "Sodomites." I apologize too for issuing strident statements following the deaths of Sonny Bono and Princess Diana, decrying their "immoral, God-defying decadence." I apologize for having authored a pamphlet titled "Mother Teresa in Hell."

I apologize for playing a tape simulating the dying screams of Matthew Shepard and for placing simulated photos of him burning in the flames of hell on my Web site.

I apologize for bringing the entire city of Topeka, Kan., into disrepute by having its name linked to mine in news reports around the world.

I apologize for indoctrinating my children and grandchildren into my own special brand of "religion," forcing them to spew and spread hatred. I apologize for responding to allegations made, by two of my sons, of wife beating and child abuse by saying, "I prefer to avoid vain and profane babblings and insolent questions by heathens."

I apologize for blackening the eye of all religions everywhere by calling myself a representative of the Westboro Baptist Church. I apologize for misappropriating, misusing, and misquoting the Bible, twisting its wonderful words to fit my warped ends.

I apologize for existing for so long as an apostle of evil.

Having confessed my sins, I am happy to say that I have seen the light. My motto has changed. No longer will I claim "God hates fags." From this day forward I will spread the good word: "God hates hate."